HAUNTED CARTHAGE, MISSOURI

HAUNTED CARTHAGE, MISSOURI

LISA LIVINGSTON-MARTIN

Haunted America

Published by Haunted America
A Division of The History Press
Charleston, SC 29403
www.historypress.net

Unless otherwise noted, all images are courtesy of the author.

First published 2013

Manufactured in the United States

ISBN 978.1.62619.204.1

Library of Congress CIP data applied for.

Notice: The information in this book is true and complete to the best of our knowledge. It is offered without guarantee on the part of the author or The History Press. The author and The History Press disclaim all liability in connection with the use of this book.

For everyone who explores these mysteries with me…you know who you are.

CONTENTS

Acknowledgements

This project has been far from a solo effort. I am grateful to many people for supporting and helping me during this process. I thank my family for understanding and helping me in numerous ways from tedious and mundane to fun and adventurous. Thank you to all of the Paranormal Science Lab team members, whose efforts made much of this project possible. Special thanks to Paranormal Science Lab team leaders, Eric Crinnian and Mistie Cole.

Thank you to those who have been supportive of Paranormal Science Lab and its efforts to bring attention to and to promote preservation efforts for historic sites, including Kendrick House in Carthage, Missouri; Burlingame & Chaffee Opera House, in Carthage, Missouri; and the Olivia Apartments in Joplin, Missouri. Thank you to Victorian Carthage, the nonprofit owner of Kendrick House, including Board of Directors members Kelly Still Harris, Bonnie Harris and Roberta Williams. Thank you to Keith and Rachel McBride, owners of the Burlingame & Chaffee Opera House. Thank you to Mark Williams of Stonesthrow Properties, LLC, owner of the Olivia Apartments. Thank you to Mike Harris, Gary Bandy, John Hacker, Joe Hadsall, Rebecca Haines, Kevin McClintock, Nikki Patrick, Blake James, the *Carthage Press*, the *Joplin Globe*, *Joplin Metro Magazine*, *Show Me the Ozarks Magazine*, the *Joplin Fuse*, KOAM TV, KODE TV and KSN TV, *Pittsburg Morning Sun*, *Neosho Daily News* and the Missouri Humanities Council for spreading the word. Thank you to all those who have attended PSL activities at Kendrick House, Olivia Apartments and the Burlingame & Chaffee Opera House, including the Haunted History Tours. We have made new friends and enjoyed sharing history and the paranormal with the public.

I am indebted to the knowledge of many people in researching and writing this book. I want to thank Steve Cottrell, author and expert on Civil War history in southwest Missouri, for insights. I also want to thank Steve Cottrell and Cliff Kester, who are both active in Civil War reenactments, for graciously posing for images that appear in this book, including appearing as our "ghostly" soldiers. I thank former and current property owners and residents of locations featured in *Haunted Carthage* for speaking with me. I learned many additional, interesting facts during these conversations. Thank you to the staff of the City of Carthage Civil War Museum; the Battle of Carthage Battlefield Park; the Bushwhacker Museum in Nevada, Missouri; the Joplin Public Library; Webb City Genealogy Society and Webb City Library in Webb City, Missouri; and the Baxter Springs Heritage Museum in Baxter Springs, Kansas.

I wish to extend a special thank-you to Janice Tremeear, author of *Missouri's Haunted Route 66: Ghosts Along the Mother Road* and *Haunted Ozarks*, for encouragement and for the introduction to my editor, Ben Gibson, and especially to Ben Gibson and everyone at The History Press for making this book a reality—a dream come true.

Spiritualism and Southern Culture

Making of Haunted Carthage

Carthage, Missouri, is steeped in a rich and intertwined history. Multiple factors came together in the vicinity of Carthage that suggest a likelihood to become a site of paranormal activity. The area that would become Jasper County, Missouri, was purchased by the federal government from the Osage Indians for $1,200 in cash and $1,500 in merchandise in 1808. White settlers, mostly southerners, came into the area beginning in the 1830s. Various settlements and towns were formed in the area, including nearby Cave Springs and Sarcoxie. Carthage quickly grew to be the largest town when Jasper County was formed in 1841. In 1842, Carthage was selected as the county seat. The town was built up around the public open square. On the north side of the square, a one-room wood-frame courthouse was built at a cost of $398.50, completed in June 1842. By 1851, the county had replaced the wooden courthouse with a two-story brick courthouse in the center of the square. The early settlers were industrious and self-reliant, and many prospered from farming and industry. Carthage quickly grew into a commercial center.

Over time, a blending of the Native American legends of the region and the southern settlers' own beliefs converged to give the Ozark Plateau region that surrounds Carthage a rich, unique folklore, including documentation of paranormal experiences. As a result, in certain places, events of long ago continue to reverberate in the form of paranormal activity. The observer is left with the task of deciphering that activity as to its origin and meaning.

Monument to the Osage War of 1837 on the courthouse lawn on the square in Carthage.

Many paranormal legends in the region have their origins in local Native American lore. From the Hornet Spook Light to the Devil's Promenade and legends of creatures such as the Goatman, Native American beliefs persist. These stories have been elaborated on over time with the experiences of settlers coming into the region. There are some recurrent ghost stories told throughout the Ozark Plateau area that date to the 1800s. There are numerous stories of old log cabins that were haunted. Often the stories center on noises heard by passersby. The distinct sounds of someone chopping wood or an axe being sharpened on a grindstone would be described, as well as the sound of water being poured on the grindstone in intervals, as would have been done in life. This story was recounted in various places and usually involved abandoned cabins and farmhouses. Other types of noises discussed in these early ghost stories include that of a man's boots walking across the floor and retrieving water from a bucket. This story was not only associated with abandoned homes but was even told by an elderly woman in the early 1900s as happening in her small log cabin where she lived by herself.

In other instances, the cabin itself was the "ghost." Phantom cabins have been observed at a distance by people in spots where no building ever existed as far as local residents can recall. These visions would appear and vanish as one approached them, almost as a mirage. Another common story would involve travelers observing smoke coming from the chimney of an unoccupied cabin, and upon inspection, they would find floors covered in thick, undisturbed dust and no evidence that a fire had been built in the fireplace in a very long time. Likewise, the phantom cabins described often included smoke coming from the chimney.

Another recurring haunting in the Ozarks involves animals, most often a large black dog. This phantom is often described as being larger than a normal dog. The dog will follow people silently and exhibit the normal movements of a dog. Some versions of the story describe the dog as headless. The significance of the dog being headless is uncertain, although early accounts usually state that the witnesses are frightened and unsettled by that fact. It appears that in certain versions, the apparition of the black dog was understood as an omen of death. A similar story arose during the Civil War, when soldiers told stories of observing a huge phantom wild boar. This apparition became associated with the death of the observer, usually within a week. One account tells of a soldier who saw the ghost boar the

Early log cabin typical in the Carthage area. The blanket would have covered a window cut out of the logs.

night before an intense battle. The night after the battle, he boasted that he had beat the curse since he survived the battle. However, he was killed that same night by the accidental discharge of a comrade's gun.

Traditionally, there was a strong belief in witchcraft in the Ozarks region as well, which contributed to a sense of fear of ghosts and haunted places as potentially evil. It was common for early settlers to take precautions against witches that may cross their paths. One such precaution was the use of a witch peg, a charm found in rural areas of the Ozarks, meant to keep witches from a home. Often they were made from cedar wood, generally used by traditional societies in Europe and by Native Americans as protection against evil spirits and negative influences. The peg had three prongs and was driven into the ground in the path to the door. Folklore held that the prongs represented the Christian Trinity. It was considered bad luck to step on or disturb a witch peg.

Vance Randolph, who was an expert on Ozark folklore, chronicled these beliefs, which persisted into the 1940s when he was writing books such as *Ozark Magic and Folklore*. Even at that time, witchcraft was commonly seen as a real threat. The danger was perceived to be ever-present and could come in the form of seemingly innocent activities such as teaching schoolchildren to say their multiplication tables backward as well as forward as a memorization tool. This was viewed by many as anti-Christian because of the belief that witches recited the Lord's Prayer backward during their ceremonies. According to Randolph, one "pious Baptist lady" in McDonald County, Missouri, disagreed with the local schoolteacher for teaching the girls in her care their multiplication tables in such a way because of the danger that "they'll be a-sayin' somethin' else back-lards tomorrow." This general atmosphere led many to avoid places known to be haunted and to speak of such things in hushed tones.

Natural features are also a source for some of the legends of haunted Carthage. It has long been speculated that in the 1600s, Spanish soldiers were lost in the Ozarks with a gold caravan on their way to Mexico. Some of these legends place the lost gold as being buried in caves in the Jasper County area. While no treasure has been found in the underground caves beneath Carthage, they have lore of their own and may have connections to haunted Carthage's present ghosts. While the cavern entrances have long been blocked off, descriptions survive that explain how the caves earned their mysterious reputation, including the account from the initial exploratory expedition on December 19, 1872, as recorded in Mills and Company's *History of Jasper County, Missouri*:

Discovery and exploration of a great cave on Garrison Avenue. A great subterranean cavern with enormous rooms and compartments. One chamber was 583 feet in extent and one passage 80 rods [1,320 feet] *in length. There was also found a clear underground lake, across which no one of the exploring party could throw. Many crystal stalagmite and stalactite specimens were found, beside numerous fossils and petrified remains of extinct animals. Truly the bowels of the earth are full of wonders as well as the heavens above, and the waters under the earth.*

Perhaps the biggest catalyst for future haunted places in Carthage was the violence that descended on the area, leaving the land scorched and nearly empty. Most would assume that it was the Civil War that brought violence to Carthage, but it was not the first war fought on this land. The Osage Indians, who had surrendered their land in 1808, returned to the area in 1837 in hunting parties. The Missouri State Militia responded and drove the hunting parties of the Osage, Shawnee and Delaware into Kansas and Arkansas after armed skirmishes. This marked the end of the Indians foraging into southwest Missouri—until involvement in the Civil War. A historical marker regarding the Osage War is on the courthouse lawn in Carthage. During the 1850s, national politics encroached on the Kansas-Missouri border, displacing work and family life as the dominant influences in the area. The Border War was a crucible along the border of Missouri and Kansas, most bitter along the southern part of the border, even years before the outbreak of formal hostilities. Why here instead of the Mason-Dixon line in the East?

The southwest corner of the Carthage square, originally a drugstore. Many of the fossils and artifacts found in the underground cavern were housed in this building for many years.

The Missouri Compromise, which allowed Missouri to enter the Union as a slave state but limited slavery in the future to south of the line along the southern border of Missouri, was an attempt to keep a balance between southern and northern states in Congress. This arbitrary line led to more strained and contorted compromises for entry of other states into the Union. For instance, the Compromise of 1850, among other things, allowed California into the Union as a free state, resulting in a majority in Congress for northern states. In 1854, it was apparent that Kansas and Nebraska would become states. The influential Illinois Democratic senator Stephen Douglas, future rival of Abraham Lincoln, engineered a solution that on first impression seemed rational: Kansas and Nebraska were allowed to enter the Union and determine their own future on the issue of slavery. However, Douglas had personal interest in ensuring the compromise was passed. He had a stake in the transcontinental railroad, then being built, and he desired that the eastern hub be Chicago, in his home state. Nebraska was not suitable to slavery due to climate and landscape, and it was along the northern emigration route, meaning it would be settled by northerners, so the ultimate route of the transcontinental railroad would safely be placed in northern territory. Although Kansas was never realistically a good candidate for widespread slave labor, it was along the same emigration route from the same southern states, as was southern Missouri. Kansas became the symbolic battleground over the future of slavery. An unintended consequence to this solution to the Kansas-Nebraska slavery issue was a clash of northern and southern culture along the Missouri-Kansas border, which would have great impact on the region in the coming war.

Abolitionists in New England set out to ensure that northerners settled Kansas and established companies, such as the New England Company, designed to solicit settlers for Kansas by the use of propaganda. This policy ignored the fact that there were a large number of people already living in the Kansas territory, including people who had held slaves in Kansas lawfully under federal law for many years. Many Missourians had made land claims in the Kansas territory. The new arrivals ignored the existing legal claims of landowners, where the preexisting owner was a southern sympathizer or owned slaves. As such, tensions mounted quickly. Soon, residents across the border in Missouri were living along an open border with settlements of radical abolitionists who were willing to impose their views on those around them, increasingly with extreme means, including raids into Missouri to liberate slaves, burning homes and murder. As the dispute over slavery spilled out of Kansas and affected Missourians directly, border retaliation soon followed. Most of the slave population in Missouri was along the Mississippi River to the east and along the Missouri River in northern Missouri. Despite that fact, the most intense border violence in this prewar period came out of

Linn County, Kansas, in the form of raids into Bates and Vernon Counties in southwest Missouri. Federal law and Kansas territorial law protected the proslavery settlers as well as the interests of Missouri residents, whose slaves had been liberated by abolitionists. The federal government tried to enforce existing legal rights of the citizens, which in the eyes of many abolitionists meant that the federal army was proslavery, leading to clashes. Federal troops enforcing the rights of the proslavery settlers in Kansas included a number of men who played key roles in the war in Missouri, including the future Confederate general Joseph Shelby and Army Scouts Buffalo Bill Cody and Wild Bill Hickok. A symbolic illustration of the change to come is the fact that the abolitionist newcomers started raiding army posts in Kansas, and in one raid during 1856, they captured a brass cannon from the Mexican War named Old Sacramento, which five years later would be used by the Federal army, commanded by Colonel Franz Sigel against the Missouri State Militia and Confederate forces, at the first large-scale land battle of the Civil War, the Battle of Carthage in southwest Missouri.

Jasper County in general and Carthage in particular were not immune from violence in this border war. The first such incident is not as clearly classified as politically motivated but rather a response to a horrific crime, although one wonders whether the punishment would have been different in the absence of the border issue. Carthage became the site of violence, culminating in the horrific deaths of two slaves at the hands of a mob, described in *History of Jasper County, Missouri* (1883):

> *In the month of March, 1854, a terrible tragedy was enacted in the southern portion of the city of Carthage, in the hollow, near Mr. Ezra Huntley's residence in which two negroes were burned to death at the stake, by the populace, for committing the threefold crime of murder, rape and arson. The particulars of the fearful crime of which they were guilty, and the terrible retribution which they suffered, are as follows: Dr. Fisk, a man highly regarded by all who knew him, had some dealings with John B. Dale, a few days before, in which he received a large sum of money. A negro belonging to Mr. Dale, named Colley, knew of the transaction, and conceived the idea of murdering the doctor for the money. He took into his confidence a colored man* [named Bart] *belonging to John J. Scott. Their plan was to entice the doctor away from his house, kill him, and then return to the house, kill the inmates, plunder the house, and then set fire to it.*
>
> *The night the horrible crimes were committed Colley went to the doctor's house, and told him Dale's child was sick, and that he should come over*

right away. The doctor, supposing that all was right, mounted his horse and started on his way. After he had gone but a short distance from the house, Bart, who was lying in wait for him, came up behind him and knocked him off his horse, and Colley came up with an ax and beat his brains out. Then they went back to the house, and after outraging Mrs. Fisk, killed her, and a child of two years of age; plundering the premises, getting only some thirty dollars in silver and a watch, which were afterwards recovered. They then fired the house and fled. This was about midnight, and none of the neighbors discovered the burning building.

They hid the plunder in a corn-crib. Colley went back to his cabin at Mr. Dale's, and Bart took to the bush for safety. In the morning… [Colley] *arose very early, went out to hunt the horses on the prairie, and in a short time returned and told the folks that Dr. Fisk's house was on fire. Someone started for the doctor's house, and before reaching it found the doctor, where he had been killed. In the ruins of the house were discovered the remains of Mrs. Fisk and child. The news soon spread, and the neighbors gathered to the scene of the crime. Suspicion at once pointed to Colley as the perpetrator. To test him, they placed him to watch Dr. Fisk's corpse. He exhibited unusual nervousness, and soon became sick and begged to be excused. He was immediately arrested and taken to Mr. Dale's house. Mrs. Dale thought he had committed the crime because he had changed his clothes. On searching his cabin his other clothing were spattered with blood. He still denied having any knowledge of the deed; and the incensed populace took him to a high gate beam and drew him up with a rope, and threatened to hang him on the spot unless he confessed what he knew. Finally, a committee, consisting of Littlebury Bedford, J.M. Jackson, and A.J. Burden, were appointed to guard him, and talk with him; and to them he confessed and gave the horrid details of the crime; and also revealed where the stolen goods were hidden, which was found to be correct.*

Bart was still at large. A large force of men turned out to search for him. Women and children of whole neighborhoods would collect at one house for safety, while the men scoured the country in search of the fugitive. Traces of the murderer were found day after day, and the circle gradually closed around him. He was ignorant of the topography of the country and being obliged to travel at night to avoid being seen, he never got beyond the boundaries of Jasper County. One evening some children discovered him skulking through the brush about a mile and a quarter south of where Georgia City is now situated [approximately three miles from the Kansas border] *and reported it to a squad of men in a house nearby.*

> *They immediately surrounded the place on horseback, and soon captured him. He was armed with a gun and pistol, but made no resistance.*
>
> *An examination was had before a committee of citizens chosen for that purpose and when all the facts were brought to light, popular indignation was almost without bounds. All were agreed that they deserved death, but there was a difference of opinion in regard to the mode. Some were for hanging them, while others insisted that hanging was too good for them, that they ought to be burned. Finally it was agreed that the mode of death should be left to a vote of the people. The vote was taken on the east side of the public square* [in Carthage], *the people dividing into two separate lines, and marching between two men stationed at the northeast corner of the square, for the purpose of being counted. After the vote was counted it was found that the proportion of those voting was two to one in favor of burning. Quite a large number of those present did not vote at all. It was then announced that they would be burned at the stake in three days from that time.*
>
> *The largest crowd ever assembled in Jasper County, up to that time, gathered on that afternoon to witness the awful spectacle. It was a very sultry day. Special pains had been taken to secure the attendance of nearly all the negroes in the county, who were given the nearest position to the stake. At three o'clock the murderers were marched out into the hollow. Thousands of spectators followed and took their position on the side of the adjacent hills. The negroes were chained between large posts, a cord or so of dry fagots were piled around them waist high, well supplied with shavings. Mr. Dale's negro stood the trying ordeal bravely, and sang songs until the flames suffocated him, but the other man pleaded piteously for release. After the fire had been kindled he screamed for them to take it away and he would tell them all about it. Two colored men lighted the fire, and as soon as the flames struck the bodies of the victims they made one or two surges and then sank down without any further struggling. In an hour the fire had burned down, and but little remained of the murderers. People from the adjoining counties had come from fifty miles to witness the sight. A heavy thunder shower came up in the evening and many got thoroughly drenched before they reached their homes.*

Public executions were common across America during this time, and while associated with the old West, public hangings would continue for decades. In Carthage, public hangings would occur both on the courthouse lawn and at the jail yard until the 1920s. The revulsion of the writer in the foregoing account was not isolated and eventually led to the movement to conduct executions behind high prison walls. The last public execution in the nation occurred in 1937 in nearby Galena, Stone County, Missouri, and is an example of the atmosphere surrounding these events, as described in the *St. Louis Post-Dispatch's Everyday Magazine*, March 20, 2001:

> *Jack Jennings' buddies beat him to the good perches in the trees. They could see over the temporary wall to the gallows on the courthouse lawn. He slipped through the crowd and found a narrow gap between two of the wall's rough-cut oak planks. He held his ground. Jennings wasn't about to miss Stone County's first and only public hanging. Jennings was 14 when Roscoe "Red" Jackson was hanged at dawn on May 21, 1937, for murdering a traveling salesman for his car and $18. Several hundred witnesses were jammed inside the temporary stockade, built around the gallows, and many more people milled about the courthouse square.*
>
> *Sheriff Isaiah H. Coin had issued about 400 written invitations to the hanging. Holding a pass was enough to get inside the 40-foot-square stockade. "I had an uncle who got in, but the kids weren't allowed," said Jennings, now 77. "I got my spot and could see them walk Red up the stairs and put the noose on him. Everybody got real quiet. The priest said some prayers and Red said something. They put the hood on him and I heard the crack of the trap door dropping. Just like that, I couldn't see him anymore. The crowd inside was just too big for me to see him go down."*
>
> *Nobody could have known it then, but they constituted the last big audience for an execution in the United States. There are some qualifiers—Owensboro, Ky., had hanged a man one year earlier without building a stockade to limit viewing…historians…cit*[e] *Jackson's as the nation's last public execution…*
>
> *Public executions were regular events during the first half of the nation's history. In the 1890s, about 90 percent of all executions were held in the county in which the offense was committed—not in state prisons. That put arrangements into the hands of sheriffs, who could make them as public as they cared to. Some executions drew special excursion trains. But by the 1920s, states had taken over 90 percent of executions…Missouri followed suit in 1938, ordering that all executions be carried out in a gas chamber at the old Missouri State Penitentiary in Jefferson City. In the same month as Jackson's hanging, the Missouri Legislature passed a law ending hangings by county and moving the executions to Jefferson City.*

> *State Sen. Paul Jones of Kennett, who was repulsed by the "carnival and Roman holiday" atmosphere of executions in his native Bootheel, pushed for the change. Newspaper editorials of the time cited growing revulsion over public hangings…*
>
> *With the noose around his neck, Jackson turned to the crowd and spoke calmly. "Well now, folks, it's not everybody that realizes what it takes to die. It's easy when it comes accidental, but it's not so easy when it comes gradual," Jackson said. "Well, be good, folks."*
>
> *A deputy covered Jackson's head with a black hood. At 6:04 a.m.,* [Mr.] *Coin pushed a lever to drop the trap. Jackson's neck snapped in the plunge. As his body was carried down the stairs, deputies cut pieces of the rope and tossed them into the crowd as souvenirs.*

As tensions increased on the Kansas-Missouri border, violence no longer was limited to a response to crime. It wasn't far from here that John Brown first came to national prominence for resisting the violence of Missouri bushwhackers who set fire to abolitionist settlements at Osawatomie, Pottawattamie and Palmyra, Kansas, in 1856. Such an instance of violence, precipitated by the tension over national politics, was the experience of a schoolteacher who came from Kansas, at nearby Sarcoxie, and in 1858 was teaching children the values of the abolition movement. After multiple warnings from the public of the negative consequences of his actions, the man still refused to cease advocating abolition. The teacher was tarred and feathered and run out of town. Sarcoxie continued to actively espouse views on the Kansas question with bold statements, as noted in *History of Jasper County, Missouri* (1883):

> *Sarcoxie was the hottest point in the Southwest at the outbreak of the Rebellion, and it had not been neutral…for several years before…First rebel flag in state-Sarcoxie. It is known that it was in existence before the commencement of hostilities, though it was not publicly displayed until on the reception of the news of the surrender of Ft. Sumpter* [sic]. *This flag was twenty-seven feet in length, and was unfurled only during the day-time, from a pole nearly 100 feet in height, for about nine weeks when the pole was cut down by Colonel Sigel's troops.*

Before the armies fired the first shots in southwest Missouri, there were calls for secession, such as Judge Chenault in Jasper County, who in May

1861 delivered public speeches on the square in Carthage, Missouri, in favor of secession, with the Confederacy's Stars and Bars flying from the flagpole on the courthouse yard. Other secession calls came from the local press and businessmen, such as C.C. Dawson, publisher of the *Southwest News*, of Carthage, Missouri, who would follow the secessionist state governor Claiborne Jackson and his troops to McDonald County, Missouri, after the Battle of Carthage and would use his printing press to print Confederate money on paper torn from the ledgers taken from county offices in the Jasper County Courthouse; and Thomas R. Livingston, a prominent miner and businessman, who owned smelters, mills and a trading post, with operations at Minersville (now Oronogo), Granby and French Point, who would serve as a prominent Confederate partisan ranger. The Kansas teacher who was tarred and feathered at Sarcoxie did not forget the transgression and, during his service in the Federal army, passed through Sarcoxie and, without fanfare, set the schoolhouse on fire. Towns along the Kansas-Missouri border were burned before the beginning of official hostilities, including Georgia City, near where the fugitive Bart was apprehended. The burnings would only continue after the war began.

During the course of the Civil War, more than 1,150 battles and skirmishes were fought in Missouri, or 11 percent of the war's total. More occurred in Missouri during 1861 than in any other state, and more occurred in Missouri during the entire war than in all other states except Virginia and Tennessee. More than 40,000 Missourians served in the Confederate army, and more than 110,000 served in the Union army. Additionally, thousands more served as partisan rangers or guerrillas, with authorized mandates from one army or the other, who operated much like privateers on the high seas had two hundred years earlier.

WAR DESCENDS ON CARTHAGE

FIRE AND DEPREDATION

The change in position of the Federal government as to whose interests would be championed upon secession of Southern states in 1861 undoubtedly played a role in the decisions to be made by Missouri governor Claiborne Jackson over the following months and affected the decision of many Federal military officers on the western border to join the Confederate army. The hope, given at least lip service, of remaining loyal to the Federal government was quickly cast aside. Shortly after Jackson's inaugural address in early 1861, the Missouri State Guard was assembled near the Federal arsenal in St. Louis. Although peaceful intentions were expressed, it was perceptively viewed by Federal army officers as a prelude to seizing the Federal arsenal in St. Louis. After the fall of Fort Sumter, President Lincoln called on governors to raise seventy-five thousand men, with Missouri's quota being four regiments. Governor Jackson's response was to declare that the request of the president was illegal, unconstitutional and revolutionary. Jackson also ordered the U.S. arsenal in Liberty, near Kansas City, seized on April 20, 1861. The Missouri State Guard was encamped at Camp Jackson, not far from the capitol at Jefferson City, in central Missouri, and Jackson brazenly named streets in Camp Jackson after Confederate leaders, such as Davis and Beauregard. Captain Nathaniel Lyon was in charge of the U.S. arsenal in St. Louis and was concerned about these events. Rumors were that munitions from Federal arsenals were being hauled into Camp Jackson. Lyon decided to assess the situation personally. He disguised himself in a dress, shawl and bonnet and, accompanied by Captain J.J. Witzig, rode in a carriage through Camp Jackson undetected. His observations led him to take immediate action.

A Union Safety Committee in St. Louis had been authorized by President Lincoln and the secretary of war to quietly raise men for defense of the city in case of attack, which allowed Union supporters to raise an army for use by Captain Lyon while letting the Rebels believe there were only a small number of soldiers in St. Louis to defend the arsenal. In mission, it served the same function as the partisan ranger and guerrilla units would after war was declared. Lyon gained approval from the Safety Committee to take preemptive action and seize Camp Jackson before Jackson's Missouri State Guard attacked more Federal installations, especially the St. Louis arsenal. Word of Lyon's plan reached General Frost of the Missouri State Guard, who replied by sending a letter of assurance that no hostile acts were intended. Lyon replied that Frost's command of the Missouri State Guard was viewed as hostile toward the Federal government; that he knew Frost was in direct communication with the Confederacy and receiving supplies from it; and that the refusal to disperse the Missouri State Guard was disobedience of the president's proclamation. Lyon demanded the immediate surrender of Frost and the Missouri State Guard, promising that the prisoners would be humanely and kindly treated. While the message was clear, it was reinforced by the fact that Lyon had already left St. Louis with six to seven thousand well-armed troops and twenty pieces of artillery before the letter reached Frost.

On May 10, 1861, Lyon surrounded Camp Jackson. Hundreds of civilians, some armed, gathered to watch what transpired, including women and children. Lyon demanded Frost's surrender. Frost, after consulting with his officers and staff, determined that resistance was unrealistic and complied. The Missouri State Guard troops were taken prisoner but were offered release on the condition that they take an oath to support the U.S. Constitution and to not take up arms against the Federal government. Only eight or ten men took the oath, the rest preferring confinement. The approximately eight hundred prisoners were marched in line toward St. Louis, enclosed on either side by U.S. soldiers. When a halt was made, large numbers of civilians would press forward, jeering. Some German American soldiers at the front of the line lost patience and opened fire. No injuries resulted, and the soldiers who had opened fire were placed under arrest. Then multiple volleys were heard from the rear of the line, and civilians, including women and children, were seen fleeing and were fired upon, with about twenty-five killed or wounded, including two women and a child.

The soldiers who fired claimed that they had been attacked by the crowd with stones and fired at the command of an officer. A regiment of German American Federal soldiers took control of Camp Jackson, and there was much agitation on the part of civilians.

U.S. general Harney, Lyon's commanding officer, approved of Lyon's actions but issued a proclamation intended to calm emotions. Two days later, the state legislature passed what was called the Military Bill, which authorized the arming of the militia. General Harney issued another proclamation declaring the Military Bill an indirect secession ordinance—ignoring the protocols used by other states that had formally seceded—and unconstitutional and void. However, he declared that he did not intend to use the soldiers in his command unless forced to do so. Under the Military Bill, Governor Jackson placed General Sterling Price in command of the Missouri State Guard. Price and Harney met in St. Louis on May 21, 1861, and signed an agreement by which management of the Missouri State Guard was turned over to Price, under Jackson's supervision, and Harney declared he had no intention of military movement that would otherwise "create excitement and jealousies." Harney issued a proclamation to the people of Missouri that the forces of the state and the Federal government were both pledged to bring about peace. Harney had signed the agreement with Price and issued the proclamation for peace without authority of the Federal government, and he was relieved of his command. In fact, Harney had already taken steps to remove Federal troops from the state of Missouri. Lyon replaced Harney in command. In the meantime, Jackson and Price, pursuant to the agreement, disbanded the state troops at Jefferson City and ordered them to go home.

The removal of Harney and replacement by Lyon hastened the confrontation that soon erupted in southwest Missouri. While it seems apparent that Governor Jackson was headed down the road to secession, but for this twist of events, General Price may well have remained a Union man, as he had been vocally opposed to secession. By his own statements, it was due to his loyalty to Missouri that he felt compelled to join the Confederate army. A second conference was held in St. Louis on June 11, 1861, in an attempt to reconcile the state and Federal positions. Lyon, newly promoted to the rank of general, was accompanied by Colonel Francis Blair and Major H.A. Conant. The state was represented by Governor Jackson, General Price and Colonel Thomas Snead. Jackson wanted to avoid the Federal government ordering enlistment of men to force the Confederate states back into the Union and advocated for a compromise, wanting both governments to agree to not recruit troops within Missouri. An eyewitness to the negotiations reported Lyon's response as:

> *Shaking his head, Lyon rose and in his measured, even, earnest tones said, "Rather than agree that my government shall concede to your government one iota of authority as to one man to be recruited, one inch of soil to be divided in allegiance or neutralized between my government and your government, I will see you, Sir* [pointing to Price], *and you, Sir* [pointing to Jackson], *and myself, and all of us, under the sod!" Then taking out his watch he glanced at it, and added: "You shall have safe conduct out of my lines for one hour. Meanwhile, you can get dinner. It is now three o'clock."*

Hurriedly dining, Jackson, Price and Snead took an express train out of St. Louis. Fearing that Lyon would pursue them to Jefferson City, they burned bridges and cut telegraph lines behind them. The next day, Jackson called into active service fifty thousand militiamen "for the purpose of repelling invasion, and for the protection of the lives, liberty and property of the citizens of the State." Lyon likewise responded one day after Jackson's activation of the militia by heading up the Missouri River on steamboats. Upon hearing of Lyon's approach, Governor Jackson and General Price left the capital on the steamboat *White Cloud*. On June 15, 1861, Lyon arrived at Jefferson City and took control of the city. With Jackson gone, the state was without a chief executive until June 30, 1861, when the Union-controlled state convention met and named Hamilton Gamble to replace Jackson.

By June 16, 1861, Jackson and Price were at Boonville with three to four thousand men. Lyon, having left men to secure Jefferson City, arrived in Boonville. General Price had taken seriously ill and left Boonville by steamboat to go to his home in Chariton County to recuperate. Governor Jackson, with Colonel Marmaduke, was left to face Lyon. The forces met near Boonville, and Lyon opened with several rounds of artillery. Jackson's men were poorly armed and not disciplined. The state troops behaved bravely in the face of the artillery but were eventually forced into retreat. Lyon had two men killed, nine wounded and one missing. Jackson had two men killed and several wounded. This was a small skirmish but the first in Missouri. By the end of 1861, Missouri was the scene of nearly half the casualties to that time.

Jackson was now in essence a Confederate government in exile. With the loss of the capital, he turned south, hoping to enlist support from the regular Confederate army in Arkansas. This decision brought the

General Nathaniel Lyon at the Battle of Wilson's Creek, as appeared in *Harper's Weekly*. The caption refers to Lyon at the Battle of Springfield, demonstrating that there was not always consistency in the references to Civil War battles. *Courtesy of Victorian Carthage, LLC, Kendrick Place collection.*

war to southwest Missouri. As for the exile government, Jackson would ultimately call a Secession Convention at the Masonic Lodge in Neosho, Newton County, Missouri, in the extreme southwest corner of the state. The convention voted to secede from the Union on October 21, 1861, and Neosho became the Confederate capital of Missouri, although Jackson spent much of the rest of the war outside Missouri until dying of cancer in Little Rock, Arkansas, on December 6, 1862. The journey to a Secession Convention and a Confederate government in exile was not played out on distant battlefields reported in newspapers weeks afterward but in the tilled fields, homes and streets of southwest Missouri, which had already become, before the outbreak of war, in former Governor Stewart's words, "desolated, and almost depopulated, from the fear of a bandit horde."

However, before exile, on July 5, 1861, some sixteen days prior to Bull Run, the North and South were clashing in southwest Missouri at the Battle of Carthage. The day before, July 4, ironically, Sigel and his troops were in Carthage, and many civilians were nervous to see the German American soldiers, referred to as "the Dutch." Sigel walked the streets speaking with citizens, trying to calm fears and tensions. Some soldiers walked to the square, where they were greeted by, among others, Union supporters, including the teenage daughters of the former sheriff, Norris Hood. One of the Hood girls had sewn a United States flag into her petticoat, and raising her skirt, she revealed the flag, presumably in defiance of the Confederate Stars and Bars being flown at Sarcoxie and in front of the courthouse in Carthage at times.

That night, Sigel camped at James Spring, on the east side of present-day Carthage, and on the bluff above the spring that overlooked the trail to Sarcoxie to the east. On the bluff stood the home of Elwood and Elizabeth (Richardson) James, for whom the spring was named. Although the Jameses were from Virginia, a slaveholding state, they were far from Southern sympathizers. The Jameses built a home on this picturesque bluff in 1842 when he was elected the first county clerk/circuit clerk and recorder of deeds of Jasper County, also relocating his mercantile business from Sarcoxie. During the 1850s and 1860s, members of the James family were active in the Underground Railroad movement, and the house and a cave above the spring were utilized as hiding places for runaway slaves on their way to freedom, usually in Kansas. Local lore holds that the cave was connected to the house by a tunnel, although no evidence to verify this legend has come to light, and such a tunnel would have been several hundred feet in length

Lisa Livingston-Martin and Kelly Still-Harris in period clothing at Kendrick House.

and would have been dug through a hillside composed of red clay and rocks. The entrance to the cave is now filled in. One of Elizabeth James's family members was John Richardson, who, at the outbreak of the war, was the publisher of a newspaper in Springfield and one of the few in southwest Missouri who supported Abraham Lincoln in the presidential election of 1860. By the summer of 1861, he was a civilian aide to Colonel Franz Sigel in the U.S. Army Volunteers and was Sigel's primary guide on July 5, 1861, at the Battle of Carthage.

The spring is now known as Carter Spring, for Dr. John A. Carter, who during the Reconstruction period built a large brick mansion on the foundation of the original James house. The Carter House still stands watch atop the bluff and is used as a private residence. It also housed the first radio station in the Carthage area (KDMO) and has been called the "Radio House." I have heard accounts from people who have visited the Carter House, which sits behind a tall, ornate iron fence and gates, that they consider it to be haunted, with feelings of being watched and odd noises.

The Crossing of Buck Branch, a print by Andy Thomas of the Battle of Carthage.

The next morning, Sigel marched north of town, and the two forces met north of Dry Fork, some eight miles north of town. Originally, General Lyon and Sigel planned on meeting and trapping Jackson's forces in a pincher maneuver, but Lyon was still more than one hundred miles north, and Sigel was vastly outnumbered by Jackson's Missouri State Guard and the regular Confederate forces under General McCullough out of Arkansas. Governor Jackson oversaw the opening shots of the battle, becoming the only sitting governor to lead troops into battle during the Civil War, albeit short-lived, as once the battle intensified, Jackson relinquished field command to General Rains. The battle began with exchanges of artillery. Jackson maneuvered to surround Sigel's smaller army, but Sigel saw the flanking maneuver and opted to retreat rather than attack and be cut off and surrounded.

The fighting turned back toward Carthage, crossing Buck Branch, and then on past Kendrick House and forded Spring River before reaching the streets of Carthage. There was fighting in the streets, and civilians were drawn into the animosities. The battle turned to urban guerrilla tactics as it became a house-to-house fight. Among those civilians witnessing the fighting was fourteen-year-old Myra Shirley, later famous as Belle Starr, who helped nurse wounded in the streets. The Shirley family, Southern sympathizers and slaveholders, had multiple tracts of land in Jasper County. John Shirley owned the Shirley Hotel and tavern on the north side of the square. None of those prewar buildings survived the war due to the town being burned multiple times. A plaque in the sidewalk commemorates the spot where the hotel was located. This was Myra Shirley's first brush with the violence of war, and it was the beginning of a series of events that led her to become the Bandit Queen, Belle Starr.

The fighting proceeded to the southeast side of town, and a final intense skirmish ensued for two and a half hours in the evening. While Sigel's troops retreated east to Sarcoxie that night, Jackson, Rains and McCullough allowed a vastly smaller force to escape with few casualties. Sigel's use of the artillery prevented a more serious defeat. One of the Union cannons was lost fording one of the various rivers that day, thought to be on an island in the middle of Spring River or Center Creek. The cannon has never been found, despite many earnest searchers' best efforts. However, river channels have changed course over the intervening 150 years, and it may have been lost at one of the other crossings. It is one remaining mystery yet to be solved. The Confederate force camped at James Spring that night, the same

Above: Present-day north side of the Carthage square. In 1861, much of the north side of the square was owned by John Shirley, father of Myra Belle Shirley, the future Bandit Queen.

Left: Plaque in sidewalk on north side of the Carthage square, commemorating the site of the Carthage Hotel, owned by John Shirley and home of the young Belle Starr, which was destroyed during the Civil War.

Monument commemorating the Battle of Carthage on the courthouse lawn on the square in Carthage.

site where Sigel had spent the previous night, and would have collected water from the spring within sight of the cave used in the Underground Railroad.

In terms of losses, the Federals had thirteen killed and thirty-one wounded, and the Confederates had twelve killed, sixty-four wounded and one missing. The Federal army retreated to Mount Vernon and then Springfield, where Sigel waited for General Lyon's arrival with much-needed reinforcements. The Confederate army took control of Carthage and areas south, including garrisons at Neosho, Granby and Newtonia.

There were prisoners taken on both sides. There were no facilities or practical means of keeping prisoners, particularly at this early juncture in the war. The experience of a unit of Federal soldiers illustrates the heated emotions that were already affecting the region. The young commanding officer was in charge of a unit of German Americans. They were taken prisoner by Jackson's men, and as they were marched through town, insults were yelled and ladies of the town walked up to the soldiers and spit in their faces, although the soldiers had made no remarks or other behavior to provoke such insults. The openly hostile treatment did not end at the edge of Carthage. The prisoners were marched to Neosho, some fifteen miles south, where McCullough was garrisoned. At that point, Jackson threatened to have the "damned Dutch" prisoners shot. The Federal soldiers later recounted that General McCullough, who was a regular Confederate officer, unlike Jackson, told Jackson that should Jackson or his men harm the prisoners, he would turn his guns on them instead. The prisoners related that they were treated well by the regular Confederate troops but could not say the same for Jackson's Missouri State Guard. As quickly became the practice, the prisoners were shortly paroled to walk to Springfield, some sixty miles away, and rejoin their command. The citizens of Neosho threatened to kill the prisoners. Their hostility was enough that General McCullough provided a military escort out of Neosho for the paroled soldiers for their safety.

With the retreat of the Union army, the publisher of the Carthage newspaper, the *Southwest News*, closed the office and took the printing press to McDonald County. Businesses in Carthage were abandoned with merchandise still on store shelves. This began the transformation of southwest Missouri into a burnt wasteland, and by war's end, the transformation was complete.

As the war progressed, guerrilla attacks, intentional fires set by both sides and neglect allowed the town to decay back into the wilderness. The town was burned to the ground in 1863, with witnesses describing the swirling smoke over Carthage as appearing like a circling wagon train. Virtually all structures were destroyed.

The two-story courthouse that became a battered shell was used by both armies and guerrillas periodically, as it gave a vantage point for miles. One Union soldier described Carthage in the later days of the war, saying that

Ruins at Cold Brook, east of Carthage. While this site dates to the later 1800s, it is illustrative of many abandoned sites in the Carthage area during the Civil War period.

Cannons were an important component in the Battle of Carthage. Colonel Sigel's Federal troops reportedly lost a cannon crossing one of the rivers during the fighting as it became mired in mud. The cannon has never been recovered. Reenactment photo.

Troops had to live off the land in southwest Missouri. At times, refugees followed troop supply columns for protection. Reenactment photo.

the stench of death was smelled before they reached town. There were so few people remaining that corpses lay on the ground where they had fallen from gunshots. A scene is described of camping on the square and a soldier inadvertently standing so that the heel of his boot was in the hollow of a human jawbone, appearing almost as a spur, causing the diarist to shudder at the comparison raised in his mind.

Firsthand accounts were summed up in *An Illustrated Historical Atlas of Jasper County, Missouri* in 1876:

> *One* [in] *five dwellings had escaped destruction. Ruins made the place unsightly. The old chimneys became the nests of owls, which hooted gloomily and forebodily over the silent and desolate scene. The deserted public square and streets, overgrown with weeds, were given up to wolves and deer, except when wandering bands of marauders, the only human visitors, would stop to feed their horses and then mount and ride away.*

This fate was not isolated in the region. One Union scout riding through Dade County, near Greenfield, reported that one could ride forty to fifty miles without seeing a living person and that the land was so barren, with farmsteads and crops burned or fallow, that he requested permission to leave southwest Missouri, as there was not enough forage to feed the horses.

Kendrick House

Antebellum Elegance and Haunting Spirits

Antebellum homes are rare in southwest Missouri due to the scorched-earth policies employed by both sides during the Civil War. The term conjures images of large plantations as are found in the Deep South. Though plantations were located along the Mississippi and Missouri Rivers in Missouri, the land in southern Missouri did not lend itself to large-scale crop farming. Nonetheless, elegant antebellum homes were built here. The oldest surviving example is Kendrick House, on the northern edge of present-day Carthage, at the intersection of Garrison Avenue and VV Highway. When built, it was considered a mansion and one of the most beautiful homes in the area. It was one of three homes in the Carthage area to survive the Civil War and is the oldest standing house in Jasper County. The house was built beginning in 1849 and completed in its current state by 1856.

When the house was built, there were no roads leading to its site. There was a trail off to the east, and the trail that would become Garrison Avenue would be forged from an Indian trail that led to Fort Scott, Kansas, and later would be part of the original Route 66. However, in the 1840s, there was nothing but prairie grass and trees outlining Spring River, several hundred yards to the south.

Sennett Rankin was drawn to this spot in the mid-1840s, building a small log cabin on the northern bank of Spring River just southeast of the house, on which he began construction but that never bore his name. A prosperous farmer with large holdings in the area, Rankin broke ground on the rolling hill above the river in 1849, as slaves tended a forty-acre field carved out of the prairie by horse and man. We have no idea what plans Sennett Rankin and his wife had when they started building what later became known as the "Mansion." After a couple years, Sennett and his wife moved back to their large farm near present-day Jasper, Missouri, some fifteen miles north, without finishing or ever living in the house. The partially constructed house was sold to Sennett's son-in-law, Thomas Dawson. Soon, the lure of gold took Dawson to California to seek his fortune. Dawson did not find gold in California. He didn't finish construction either and never lived in the house. Perhaps as a means of recouping his losses from that search for gold, Dawson sold the still unfinished house and 640 acres of future farmland and orchards to William and Elizabeth Kendrick for the sizeable sum of $7,000 in 1856. At the same time in Jasper County, farmland was selling for approximately $1.25 an acre ($800 for 640 acres). The Kendricks finished the house on the hill and made it their home. They turned the 640 acres of virgin prairie grass into cropland and orchards and operated a successful blacksmithing and gunsmithing business for many years. The Kendrick family and their descendants, including several generations of the Janney family, lived in the home continuously for approximately 130 years, until it was sold to Victorian Carthage in the 1980s, which still owns the home. Approximately 20 acres of the original 640 acres remain with the house.

Kendrick House, Carthage. Built in 1849, it is the oldest standing home in Jasper County.

Lisa Livingston-Martin and Mistie Cole, Paranormal Science Lab team leaders, in front of Kendrick House. *Courtesy of Paranormal Science Lab. Jordyn Cole, photographer.*

Victorian Carthage is a nonprofit group that has as its purpose the preservation and maintenance of Kendrick House as a living museum. Victorian Carthage restored the home in the 1980s to the appearance it would have had in the mid-1800s. Care was taken to use colors, patterns and materials that are representative of the period. For instance, the wallpaper patterns in the home are consistent with those used in the mid-1800s. The wide-plank wood floors appear a pinkish-red color. While they are painted with ordinary house paint today, when first built, the planks were painted with hand-mixed paint tinted with oxen blood to give it the pinkish-red color. The woodwork you see in the house is original, and most is solid walnut from trees felled on the property. The woodwork was hand cut and hand finished by carpenters laboring on site. The limestone windowsills as well as the limestone slabs in the fireplaces and hearths are native limestone or "Carthage marble" quarried just over the hill to the west on what was originally part of Kendrick farm but later became the Carthage Marble quarry. The limestone is hard enough to be polished and in that state is referred to as Carthage marble; it has been used for numerous buildings throughout the state and nation, including the Missouri State Capitol in Jefferson City, Missouri.

Although the city of Carthage had been established by the time Kendrick House was built, it was still a small collection of houses and buildings. It was not readily accessible from Kendrick House, as there were no bridges across Spring River or in all of Jasper County until the 1870s. Everything that was used in construction of the house except for glass for the windows was either material found on the property or items that were made by the workers. For instance, there were no store-bought nails available, so each nail was made by hand by a blacksmith in a forge. The outer walls are red brick, made from the clay from the banks of Spring River, just a few hundred yards from this spot. Sennett Rankin, as well as Dawson and the Kendricks, owned slaves. Rankin was the largest slaveholder in Jasper County, and his slaves built the brick walls. The bricks are concave on the interior side so as to hold more mortar. The exterior walls are three bricks thick, very unusual for construction of the time in the region, where a small log cabin with a hole cut out of one of the logs for a year-round open window was a symbol of permanence. The thickness of the walls meant that the house was better insulated than most buildings of the time. If you look closely, you will find bricks with areas of gray glazing, which was caused when a brick was too close to a hot spot in the wood-fired kilns.

The house is Federal-style architecture, which means that there is an entryway and staircase with symmetrical wings on either side. Although the house looks large from the outside, the original structure consists of four rooms: the dining room and parlor on either side of the entryway on the ground floor and two bedrooms on the second floor. There was no running water in the home until 1954. Water was originally available from the hand-dug well beside the house and a cistern that collected rainwater. There were various outer buildings on site, including a kitchen, slave quarters, blacksmith shop, smokehouse, barns and, later, homes for family members and rental homes for men working in the nearby quarry. The old outhouse still stands out back near the slave cabin. The original slave quarters were brick, like the house, but were demolished sometime in the past. The slave quarters on site were moved from the Miller, Missouri area when Victorian Carthage opened Kendrick House to the public. There have been reports of an African American man wearing a white shirt standing and looking out one of the windows in the slave quarters, staring off into the distance. The sound of harmonica music has been recorded in the slave quarters as well.

Kendrick House drew in people even before the Civil War, known as a stopping point for settlers heading west, where they engaged the

A glimpse of antebellum living in the parlor at Kendrick House. Reenactment photo.

blacksmithing and gunsmithing services of William Kendrick and his son Joshua, as well as obtaining supplies and food for their journey. It was considered a mansion for several reasons. First, it was brick and large compared to the log cabins that were standard accommodations for the area. It was outfitted with a full complement of glass windows. Glass had to be hand blown and was a luxury item and quite expensive. It also was not available locally and had to be shipped in from St. Louis, overland by oxen wagon. Imagine crossing nearly four hundred miles of natural brush, prairie and rivers without any graded roads and few bridges—all while trying to keep panes of glass from breaking. That is why houses of the period had shutters—not to keep wind or sun out but to protect the glass from breaking. A broken window meant months of exposure to the elements until it could be replaced. As glass became more common and was available locally, the expense came down, and shutters were no longer a necessity. Photos of Kendrick House taken in the 1890s show that the shutters were in disrepair and some had fallen off the house. Hand-blown glass is made by the craftsman blowing through a glass tube; the air then causes the molten glass to change shape. A consequence of the process was that air bubbles would form in the glass as it cooled and hardened. There are original hand-blown panes of glass in the cabinets in the dining room.

Springfield, Missouri, served as a jumping-off point heading west in southern Missouri. Many wagons would stop at Kendrick House or farther south at the Ritchey House in Newtonia, Missouri, for supplies and water. At Kendrick House, pioneers could obtain goods ranging from bullets to horseshoes to guns. They could also purchase food grown by the Kendricks and produce from their orchards. For many, Kendrick House was the most impressive house they had come into contact with in hundreds of miles. The house also served as a community sick house in the days before hospitals or doctors. People who were seriously ill would be brought to Kendrick House to be cared for until they recovered or passed away. It is unknown how many people died in the house over the years, but it could be considerable, as outbreaks of diseases such as smallpox, malaria and tuberculosis were recurring perils.

With the Kansas state line only twenty miles away, it was only a matter of time before the hostilities in Kansas intruded on the Kendricks' lives. On the Kendrick farm, tranquility and a lifetime of labor were interrupted on July 5, 1861, when the first large-scale land battle of the war unfolded yards from their front door. Federal troops engaged Jackson at Dry Fork about eight miles north of the Kendrick farm, with fighting coming south and passing along the trail just west of the house, now Garrison Street. Family accounts of the battle say that troops moved south toward Spring River just yards west of the house, causing the men to drop tools and run from the fields in which they were working. During the course of the day's fighting, Kendrick House was commandeered by Union troops as a hospital, and during the days after the battle it served as a field hospital for Confederate wounded as well.

Kendrick House witnessed its share of brutality from occupation by both armies and raids from bushwhackers. The Kendricks' slave woman was tortured and hanged by Confederate guerrillas who believed she was hiding a Union soldier. These same guerrillas also tortured the slave woman's young daughter, Rose, and left her for dead. After the guerrilla raiders left, the family nursed Rose back to health. Rose elected to stay at Kendrick House after the war and worked for the Kendrick family until her death at age ninety-two.

It was common in southwest Missouri for guerrilla fighters as well as regular troops to come to a house and take food and other supplies and livestock, torch crops and buildings and often kill the man of the house. It was not uncommon for the wife and children to recognize members of the lynching party as neighbors and former friends. Some of the Kendricks' close neighbors suffered this fate, including one man shot sixteen times on his front porch before he could say a word. As a consequence, the Kendricks cut a trapdoor into the floor of the parlor, covered by the rug. The family could hide under the house until danger had passed.

Bushwhackers and raiding parties from both armies were a constant threat to the safety of the civilian population in southwest Missouri during the Civil War. Reenactment photo.

The old Rankin log cabin on the bank of Spring River was occupied by distant Kendrick family members by the name of Ennis. Bushwhackers came through looking for money and valuables. Mr. Ennis was shot dead. Convinced that Mahilia Ennis was hiding money, the bushwhackers tortured her by burning her feet in a fire, to no avail, as she had no money. The men rode on, but Mrs. Ennis was left crippled, unable to ever walk again. The Kendricks brought her to the mansion, and she lived there the rest of her life, helping to care for the Kendrick grandchildren after Joshua's wife, Elvira, died. Another close call occurred when bushwhackers set fire to the front porch. Horses were hitched to the porch, and the burning timber was pulled away from the house. The family did not rebuild the porch as a reminder of what had happened. Victorian Carthage rebuilt the porch as it originally appeared more than 120 years later.

Confederate general Joseph Shelby used the Kendrick farm as his headquarters and camp in 1863 as he pushed back into Missouri. Kendrick House still bears witness to this presence. A large number of horses was a sign that soldiers were present, so often the horses were brought inside a building to conceal them from notice. Wanting the horses ready to ride in a hurry, they were boarded in the Kendricks' parlor, where built-in cabinet drawers served as troughs and the horses ate corn gathered from the family's fields. The family kept some of the ears of corn they found when the soldiers departed, and they can be seen by visitors now, still stored in the parlor. The horses also left hoof prints in the wood floor near the fireplace where they stamped their feet. Again, the family left the floor as it was as a reminder of the past.

It has been speculated that the Kendrick family, despite Confederate leanings, was able to avoid much of the brutal violence, burning and plunder suffered by most of their neighbors due to their profession as blacksmiths and gunsmiths; their services were valuable to the troops and bushwhackers who came through, so they were more valuable alive than dead as long as they didn't provoke violence. However, William Kendrick, then sixty-five years old, came very close to death at the hands of Union soldiers in late 1864. In the course of carrying out the Federal General Order Number 11—which mandated that all men in southwest Missouri known to have Southern sympathies, or who had not taken the oath of allegiance to the Federal government, vacate the region—a Union unit came to Kendrick House looking for Joshua, known to be a Southern sympathizer.

Joshua and other men had been warned of the approaching soldiers while he was away from home. He decided to head to Newton County for safety.

Despite repeated attempts, the Confederates never regained control of southern Missouri after the defeat at Pea Ridge, Arkansas, in 1862. Reenactment photo.

Troops often commandeered homes, food and other supplies from the civilian population, causing more hardship and inflaming hostility. Reenactment photo.

The commanding officer demanded William tell them where his son was, but the elder Kendrick was quite deaf and couldn't hear what the man had said. Frustrated, the commander drew his pistol, put it to William's head and pulled the trigger. William's wife, Elizabeth, rushed forward and placed her thumb under the hammer of the gun, preventing it from firing and saving her husband from a gunshot to the head. The commander became enraged and wildly threatened to kill the Kendricks. His men, appearing embarrassed, pulled him out of the house, with the commander yelling that he would return and kill the whole family. His men apologized to Elizabeth, saying the commander was just drunk and they wouldn't be back. The family abandoned their home and followed Joshua to Neosho, where they stayed for the last seven months of the war.

The end of the war marked the resumption of normalcy, and the Kendricks thrived, adding businesses over the years, from a mill to a general store and gas station. The house continued to be used as a sick house for years after the Civil War and was used as the Jasper County Courthouse at times after the war and before a new courthouse was constructed on the square almost thirty years later.

Death was a frequent visitor to the Kendrick-Janney family. Three of William and Elizabeth's sons died while the Civil War raged around the family: Richard, Alex and Austin, all in their early twenties. William passed

Portrait of Elizabeth Kendrick that hangs in Kendrick House.

away in 1868, followed by Elizabeth in 1878. Joshua's wife, Elvira, followed in death in 1884. Joshua and Elvira's daughter, Fannie, with her husband, Carl Janney, raised their family in the mansion. Tragedy struck again in 1899, when Fannie and Carl's four-year-old daughter, Pauline, died in the house of an unspecified spinal disease. Joshua died in 1901, and Fannie inherited the house and farm.

The last person to die in Kendrick House was Carol Sue Janney, Fannie and Carl's granddaughter, who lived in another house on the family land at the time. Carol became ill on or about April 23, 1936, a few months short of her third birthday. To protect her four-year-old sister, Jackie, from contracting the illness, Carol was brought to the mansion. A doctor was summoned, and it was discovered she had contracted polio, for which there was no vaccination or cure at the time. Approximately thirty-six hours after becoming ill, little Carol died in the big house.

It is here that Paranormal Science Lab (PSL) conducts Haunted History Tours and paranormal investigations, raising funds for preservation efforts at Kendrick House. Historic homes such as Kendrick House face very difficult obstacles to maintain the property and keep the doors open to the public. Victorian Carthage and Paranormal Science Lab have worked together to raise awareness of the history of the house, as well as offering people an opportunity to experience a real-life paranormal investigation. People have traveled from across the United States, as far away as California and Georgia, to attend Haunted History Tours and paranormal investigations. Tours focus on the history of the house and Civil War history of the area. Guests review evidence of paranormal activity documented at Kendrick House by PSL and then participate in a live investigation. Proceeds are donated to Victorian Carthage for preservation efforts. PSL members also donate labor to Victorian Carthage to make repairs and maintenance. The Missouri Humanities Council, which, among other things, promotes public awareness of history and works with museums and historic sites to provide educational experiences for the public, has used the Haunted History Tours offered at Kendrick House as an example of combining the interest in history and the paranormal for fundraising at historic sites.

PSL has been fortunate in being able to conduct extensive research at Kendrick House, building a large body of data that allows the group to conduct continuing experiments based on scientific principles, with the long-term goal of explaining the cause and nature of paranormal activity observed at Kendrick House and other sites. More information about tours, Paranormal Science Lab's investigation methods and examples of evidence collected can be found at the PSL website (www.paranormalsciencelab.com) and on Facebook (www.facebook.com/PSLMissouri).

There is a modern addition on the back of the house used as part of the museum. The original frame-structure kitchen, which was behind the west end of the house, is long gone. The purpose of locating the kitchen outside the main structure was for safety. Cooking was done on open hearths and ovens with wood fires. Kitchen fires, including catching floor-length skirts on fire, were one of the most common causes of injury and death to women of the mid-nineteenth century. The kitchen also contains a large long room with various artifacts found on site from the 1800s. The room is dominated by a long, narrow dining table that is original to the house and, according to family lore, was used as the field hospital operating table during the Battle of Carthage. This was merely lore until Paranormal Science Lab employed techniques used in crime scene investigations to supply corroboration of the story. As demonstrated on crime investigation television shows, law enforcement uses UV (ultraviolet) light to search for bloodstains. Paranormal Science Lab approached the table as a crime scene. Blood appears violet or purple under UV light. It is extremely difficult to eliminate all traces of blood, even after long periods of time. Turn out the lights and turn on UV flashlights, and the ordinary, antique table takes on a vastly different appearance. At one end there are violet spots in splatter patterns, and as the UV passes down the length of the table, lines of violet illuminate the grain of the wood planks forming the tabletop and violet drips down the side edges and legs. Although a bit macabre, it makes perfect sense. A military field hospital of the 1860s could be anywhere from a tent to a barn to a house commandeered, as was Kendrick House. A long table worked well, and one end would be propped up so that fluids would run off into buckets or bowls at the other end. The UV test supports the family lore handed down through more than 150 years that this table saw a lot of blood and thus very likely is the operating table used by army doctors during and after the Battle of Carthage.

Still image of Kendrick House kitchen area taken with a camera on a tripod from the adjoining room; the field hospital operating table is in the foreground on the right. *Courtesy of Paranormal Science Lab. Brian Schwartz, photographer.*

This photo was taken eight seconds after the previous photo. No one was in the kitchen, despite the shadow. *Courtesy of Paranormal Science Lab. Brian Schwartz, photographer.*

A large number of EVPs (electronic voice phenomena) have been recorded in the room where the table now sits, which is in an addition that did not exist in 1861. It is believed that the table does sit in the general location of where the operations were performed, as the room sits directly behind the original back door to the house. It was a very hot day on July 5, 1861, and no evidence of bloodstains have been found inside the house, so it is likely that the table was carried out the back door and set up as an operating table. EVPs are voices captured on audio that were not audible to those present at the time of recording. Many are at frequencies outside the range of the human voice. EVPs have been captured in the room containing the operating table that seem to be related to the Civil War period, including one that says "General — E Lee" and another that names Peter Hahn, a German name. The Union troops headquartered at Kendrick and working and bleeding in the field hospital were mostly German Americans. The EVP captured says "Peter Hahn's wish" and occurs as PSL conducts a Haunted History Tour and the story of the operating table being tilted to allow fluids to flow to one end is being told. Is it possible that a Peter Hahn was present in the field hospital? Additionally, there is the ironic fact that the name Peter Hahn is associated with the set of medical texts *A Practice of Medicine*, which were the official reference books of Union and Confederate army surgeons and written by George Bacon Wood, Peter Hahn's son-in-law. Is there a connection to his name being heard around the operating table? During investigations, people have lain on the operating table, and many report feeling as if their arms and/or legs are being held down. Some report having pain, usually in a leg or in the side. And a few have become disoriented and ill, having to excuse themselves to vomit. Curiously, it has been only men who have become ill—whether because it would have been men lying on the table experiencing Civil War surgery is an interesting possibility.

Other interesting activity in this room is the sound of a hammer hitting an anvil that is heard. Also, the sounds of heavy bootsteps, followed by the distinct sound of a screen door opening and closing, is heard in the vicinity of the doorway that was the original back door to the house. At times, the bootsteps are followed by a man sighing heavily. In the adjoining hallway, shuffling footsteps are a regular occurrence.

Numerous EVPs have been captured in this area. Two men have been heard in the midst of conversation. A young girl's laughter is heard. EVPs of a woman's voice calling for Tom are a frequent occurrence as well. I even had a PSL team member hear a woman's voice say, "Hello Lisa," on one occasion. Another EVP in this area is unexpected. As two female investigators and a male investigator walked through the room past the operating table, a male voice said, "I must kiss her." Interestingly, one of the women in the room had not been in the house previously. Whether this was an intelligent interaction or residual activity, replaying an event from the past, is unknown. Another significant experience in this part of the house is the sighting of shadow people. Shadow people are believed by some to be nonhuman entities. Others believe them to be apparitions akin to the traditional notion of a human ghost but without features or color. A shadow person has been captured on camera multiple times in the area near the doorway between the kitchen and the room with the operating table. In the foyer, a shadow person has been captured on video, in very childlike behavior, as if playing peekaboo. Attempts to duplicate these images by re-creating them with shadows of people have not been successful.

The first floor is also where balls of lights are seen and have been caught on video. They appear as three-dimensional spheres with texture and uneven

Parlor at Kendrick House. General Joseph Shelby and his staff boarded their horses in this room, feeding them corn from the Kendricks' fields out of the cabinet drawers. Still visible are the horses' hoof impressions in the floorboards by the cabinets from stamping their feet.

surfaces that change as they move through the air, with an ever-changing intensity of brightness, reminiscent of plasma. Guests on tours have also captured photos with anomalies that are not readily explained by natural or man-made factors. Many people believe that orbs, opaque circular objects appearing in photographs, are ghosts or entities. PSL does not ascribe to that theory. Virtually all such objects appearing in a photograph are dust particles, pollen or moisture suspended in the air. These particles are actually within inches of the camera lens. When taking pictures, you can eliminate almost all such orbs by using a sun filter.

As you enter the parlor, you can see the trapdoor that leads under the house. There are legends of tunnels leading away from the house. Although no evidence of tunnels has been discovered, in recent years, volunteers at the house have been told by elderly men touring the home that they played in the tunnels as children with the Janney children. Bright lights have been observed in the parlor when no one was in the house. I can attest to this fact, as one night while standing on the front lawn talking after an investigation, I and two other investigators observed what appeared to be a light begin to shine from a point below the level of the windows, approximately six feet off the ground, and brighten over two to three seconds until it was as bright as daylight, filling the room and then shrinking as quickly and disappearing before we could reach the windows. People report seeing shadows moving across windows, as if people are walking around the room, when the house is empty. This is consistent with reports from neighbors and passersby who have for decades reported seeing various apparitions in the yard. In front of the house, a man in a Civil War uniform is seen, as well as a tall man in a white shirt and trousers who stands near the old well. Most intriguing, however, is the apparition of a young girl in a plaid dress who has not only been seen near Kendrick House but has also been reported walking across a pasture toward a neighbor's house and seen entering the neighbor's back door. Afterward, unusual activity occurred in the neighbor's house, such as moved objects and doors opening on their own. After a while, the neighbor announced, "All right, you've played enough. Time to go home." The neighbor stated that the odd activity ceased, and shortly thereafter, a light came on in Kendrick House, even though no one was present.

Thermal images taken of the parlor windows have captured a cold signature of what appears to be a woman sitting on one of the windowsills in the parlor. Children in period clothing have been observed playing with a ball in the backyard at night, causing witnesses to relate their experiences in shaken, nervous voices.

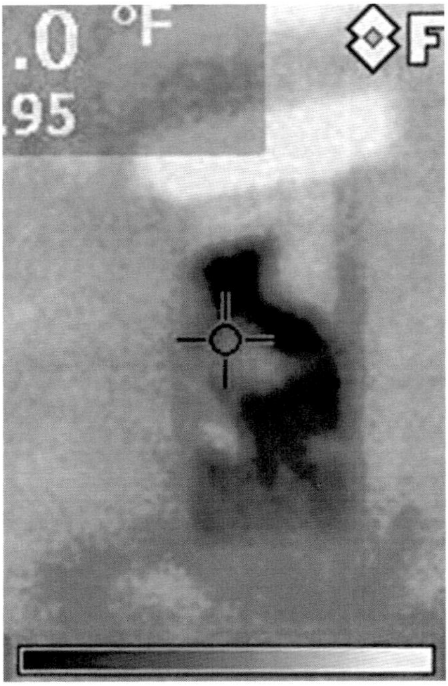

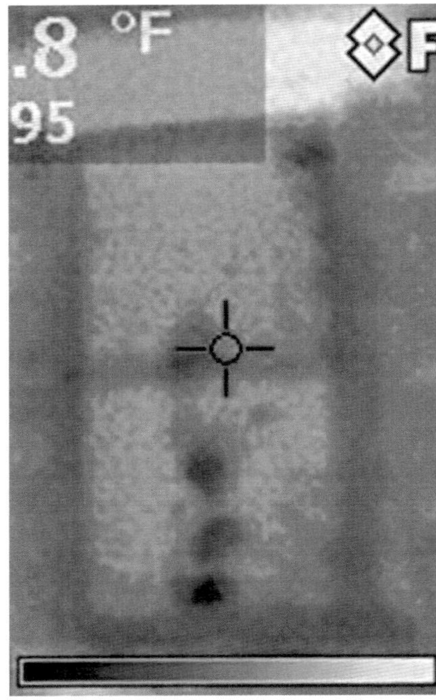

Left: A FLIR (forward-looking infrared) thermal image taken of the west parlor window from the outside. The dark area that resembles a woman sitting on the windowsill is the coldest area in the frame and descends down past the window onto the brick wall itself. *Courtesy of Paranormal Science Lab.*

Right: This image was taken approximately eight seconds after the previous image. *Courtesy of Paranormal Science Lab.*

As you proceed into the kitchen, various artifacts are displayed that give insight into antebellum southwest Missouri life. Included are utensils and a set of old skeleton keys, to which no one knows what they fit. We have to return to the story of Rose, the slave girl who was attacked and left for dead when her mother was hanged in the orchard by Confederate guerrillas. As discussed earlier, the family lore said that Rose was nursed back to health by the family and continued in their employment after the war until her death in her nineties. There is documentation that supports this claim. Newspaper columnist and local resident Arthur Grundy recounted the story of Rose in an article, "Keeper of the Keys," which was reprinted in a collection of his writings:

> *When entering Carthage, one is under the impression Spring River flows through town with a part of Carthage north of the river. The truth however is that all on the north side of the river is an entirely separate town called*

Kendricktown. If you ever visit our town, you will see a large weather-worn red brick house with a bit of ivy clinging to it. This is known as the Kendrick House—of an early day settler and slave owner. It was on this early day estate that a cute and winsome little girl was born into slavery and it was here [s]*he lived her entire life. While it is true this little girl was born a slave—it is also true that she may have known more freedom than many of us have in our modern day lives. She was free to roam the river bottom fields as a child and the valleys of the uplands covered with wild roses, which she was very fond of, as this little girl's name was Rose. She also had the advantage of being loved by the colored folk and her white master and mistress alike. Rose grew into womanhood and there was a young man in her life by the name of George. It's not clear where George came from—perhaps he also was born on this same farm, or it may have been that he was sold to the Kendrick family while he was just a young lad. At any rate Rose and George became man and wife. It's also not clear whether they were married by a legal ceremony or if it was a common-law marriage. It seems to the writer this marriage was made in Heaven and legality would be only a minor fact of this story. These two slaves were faithful servants to their master and mistress and received kindness and love in return. It's told that when their mistress was on her death bed, Rose wept and held her in her arms. A white member of this family remonstrated and begged Aunty not to die in the arms of a slave, but Aunty loved Rose and rebuked this member of her family. She said Rose had what many people in this world did not possess—"a heart of gold." God made all of us to be born and then as the years pass to grow old. This also happened to Rose and George and when they could no longer work in the fields or care for the family mansion their kindly master gave these dearly*

This set of keys has been hanging in the kitchen area at Kendrick House longer than living memory. Perhaps these are Rose and George's keys. Interestingly, EMF spikes have been detected around the keys, even in different rooms in the house. *Courtesy of the Alex Martin.*

> *loved old slaves a feeling of importance by letting them carry the keys to the barns and house. It was their chore to lock the doors each night and unlock them each morning. They became the keepers of the keys. After the Civil War a small town grew around this stately old brick house and was named after its owner—becoming known as Kendricktown. Today this is a town filled with laughing children, flowers and gardens. The keys that Rose and George carried for so many years now hang in the weather-worn red brick house. The writer lives on the outskirts of this town and even at this extreme edge there is a feeling of safety and security. This is a feeling that could only come from above, as though God has done very much like Rose's and George's earthly master and gave them the feeling of importance of watching over our safety. It's a feeling that these two faithful old slaves are still, even though they have been in heaven these many years—KEEPERS OF THE KEYS.*

Contrary to popular belief, the sentiment and affection of slave owners toward their slaves was not unusual in antebellum Missouri. It was not an unusual occurrence for slaves to be buried in family cemeteries along with family members. It is believed that Rose is still at Kendrick House, as EVPs of what sounds like an African American woman have been captured, appearing to care for children, saying such things as, "Come along now, shhh." The dining room seems to be the domain of Rose and Elvira Kendrick, the wife of Joshua, who was the first woman to raise young children in the home. EVPs indicate positive responses when asked if Elvira is present. In all, up to twelve distinct voices have been documented through EVPs in the house.

The most moving experiences reported are connected with little Pauline Janney and Carol Sue Janney. The image of Pauline has been seen on the staircase, but she seems to sit by one of the windows in the upstairs east bedroom most often. On one occasion during an investigation, while taking photographs with a thermal imaging camera, Pauline seems to have made her presence known in multiple ways. A thermal imaging camera registers the temperature range in an image through color variation, with the coldest objects appearing the darkest and the hottest objects appearing the lightest in color. In a series of images taken while standing on the brick patio at the rear of the house, a hot spot formed in the lower right-hand corner of one of the bedroom windows. The camera registered the hot spot as being ten degrees warmer than the rest of the glass. There was no one in the house at the time. The hot spot manifested within about twenty seconds over a series of five images. Without a readily apparent explanation, an

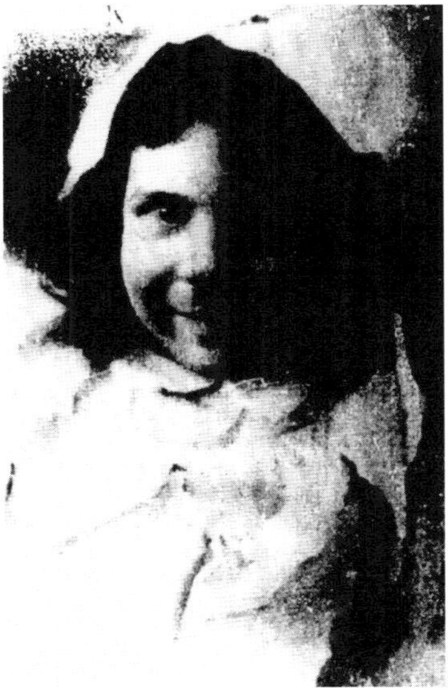

The only known image of Pauline Janney, who died at the age of four in 1899. *Courtesy of Kelly Still-Harris.*

The bedroom window where Pauline has been seen standing. This is also the curtain most often disturbed while no one is in the house.

investigator was sent upstairs to place his hands on the inside of the window glass to monitor any increase in temperature. After a full five minutes, no color change was viewed on the thermal imaging camera and no temperature change on the glass was recorded by the camera. It was also noted that the window is double paned with approximately four inches of space between the two glass panes. No explanation was found for the hot spot registered. The supposition that the hot spot was paranormal based was reinforced later that evening during a public Haunted History Tour. A woman and her aunt were walking around the grounds before the tour started and reported that while standing in the backyard, they saw a young girl standing at the window in which the hot spot had been documented. The witness described the girl as appearing about six years old, with dark hair and wearing a white dress or gown. I showed the woman a photo of Pauline, to which her reply was, "Oh my god, that's her." While not definitive, it seems that Pauline's spirit was present and interacted with the environment in the form of a temperature change as well as being seen. Also, a common event in the house involves curtains being moved, particularly in the bedrooms upstairs. This occurs so frequently that upon leaving the house, tour guides check the curtains to make sure they are hanging straight. Upon returning, approximately half the time, at least one curtain will have been moved, usually with one corner pulled back and resting on the windowsill, as if someone has pushed it aside to look out.

The curtain in the window in the east bedroom in which Pauline was seen and the hot spot was recorded is the one most often moved. Most eerie was one occasion when that curtain was found pushed back from the corner in which the hot spot formed and the lace fabric was bunched up on the windowsill in a mound. However, there were four perfectly formed indentations in the folds of lace the size of a small child's fingers. Attempts were made to reproduce the indentations, but the lace curtain would just fall in a loose fold. This exercise has been repeated on multiple occasions with the same result. It was concluded that the chances of a person replicating the indentations in the curtain are very unlikely. It is believed that it is Pauline who plays with the curtains as she watches from the windows. There have also been reports of seeing a curtain move from people driving by the house or standing on the front lawn.

Another little girl makes herself known to visitors at Kendrick House. As previously noted, in April 1936, Carol Sue Janney contracted polio, for which there was no cure at that time. She was taken to Kendrick House, and within thirty-six hours, she had succumbed and passed away. Carol seems to have stayed in the house. People are drawn to her painting in the entryway, that of a cherub-faced toddler dressed in a red coat and matching hat with

This corner of the east bedroom is frequently the site of unexplained odors such as tobacco or sweat, as if of someone who has been working strenuously.

a solemn look, as if showing her displeasure at sitting still. Where Pauline is seen at the window and on the stairs, Carol is not seen but heard. Audible gleeful laughter of a little girl is heard in the house. There have been instances when this squealing laughter has been heard in one part of the house while a girl's voice is captured on audio recording in another room. One example in particular is compelling. Two investigators were sitting in the parlor downstairs while all other investigators in the house were upstairs in the west bedroom, or children's room. An EVP session was being conducted in the children's room. The investigators in the parlor were sitting quietly when they heard a little girl squealing playfully. They climbed the stairs following the noise they heard and walked to the doorway of the children's room. On audio in the bedroom, they are heard coming up the stairs and asking if anyone else heard a child's laughter. No one had heard laughter, but just before the investigators react to laughter downstairs, the question was asked upstairs, "What is your name?" No audible response was heard; however, upon review, a child's voice responds on audio.

Multiple investigators reviewed the audio of the response to "What is your name?" There was a difference of opinion. All but one person heard "Carol." The other investigator heard "Carrot." This seemed strange to all, including the investigator who heard "Carrot." Why would a spirit say

Painting of Carol Sue Janney, the last person known to have died in the house at the age of two years and nine months.

The children's bedroom at Kendrick House.

carrot? However, he insisted he heard a hard consonant at the end of the word. A couple weeks later, evidence from that investigation was presented to the board of directors of Victorian Carthage. Prefacing the playing of the Carol/Carrot EVP, the investigator who heard Carrot explained the division of opinion by saying, "Everyone heard Carol, except me, and I heard Carrot." We received an unexpected reaction as the directors looked at one another with widened eyes. The Carrot proponent assumed they thought Carrot was a ludicrous statement and continued, "I know it doesn't make sense, but I hear a hard 'T' at the end." Wide-eyed expressions turned to smiles. One of the directors explained that Carol's sister Jackie couldn't say Carol Sue, so she called her little sister "Carrot Soup," and "Carrot" was the family nickname for Carol. We had not been told that fact before and had no way of knowing that Carrot could be significant.

Another interesting experience involving Carol occurs during EVP sessions that have lasted up to seven hours of continuous responses. At times, flashlights will be used, and while not classified as evidence, they are used as prompts in lines of questioning. However, at Kendrick House, repeated responses on four or five flashlights at once are not uncommon, with internal consistency with questions asked in different ways over a period of hours. Control experiments have been conducted where flashlights are placed in two separate rooms, with cameras monitoring activity and investigators staying in another part of the house watching on monitors. There have been times when the flashlights in one room will go on and off in patterns and then suddenly cease activity, only to commence activity in the other room and continue alternating without activity ever occurring simultaneously in both rooms. After an investigation, a video of excerpts of internally consistent flashlight responses was shown to the board of directors, and two flashlights were placed on the table near the computer playing the video. To everyone's surprise, the flashlights began turning on and off in unison to the flashlight responses on the video and continued to do so for the duration of the video.

Cold spots are often associated with paranormal activity, the theory being that the entity draws energy from the atmosphere in order to manifest or interact with the living, with a resulting drop in temperature. This phenomenon is experienced at Kendrick House. Cold spots can be large enough to cover a large section of a room or as localized as the sensation of a child wrapping her arm around your leg. One evening in the parlor, five investigators were seated around the room when one investigator had the unexpected sensation of a small child crawling up onto his left leg, and his left leg and left arm felt icy cold. A laser themomerter confirmed that

Many of the items in Kendrick House are original to the house and family, and the house is preserved as it would have appeared in the mid-1800s.

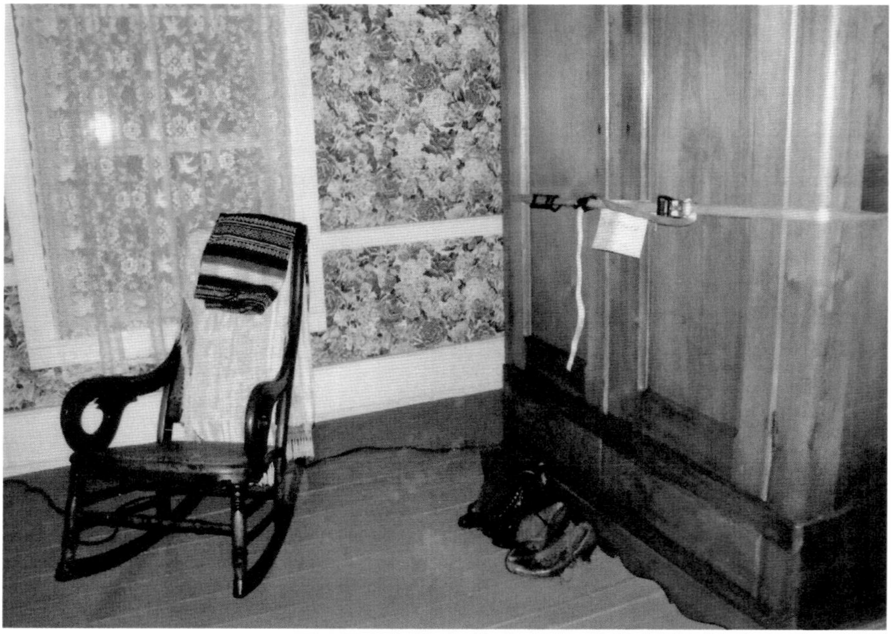

The personal items present in the house offer a firsthand glimpse into life in the 1800s. This rocking chair has been reported rocking by itself.

his left arm and leg were eight degrees cooler than his right. In case there was a draft, everyone rotated their seating positions. When he sat down again, he said he felt warmer, but a few seconds later, he visibly shuddered and said the coldness returned, again as if a child were sitting on his left leg. This was repeated as everyone in the room moved to the next available seat, and each time the cold sensation returned in the same way, and each time it was confirmed that the temperature on his left side was eight to ten degrees lower than on his right side. When the musical chairs had returned him to his original seat, the affected investigator accidentally dropped the flashlight he was holding and leaned forward to pick it up off of the floor. As he did so, a look of surprise came over him, and he said, "Wow," then relayed that a rush of cold air had rushed up around his face and neck as if he had received a hug.

Other childlike behavior comes out with trigger objects that would be familiar to children of days gone by, particularly toy balls. The floor of the children's room has been measured with a level and even had the contours taped off to determine the location of the low spots in the room. An ordinary child's rubber ball can demonstrate kinetic energy as it is rolled across the floor. At times when done in this room occupied by so many children over the years, the ball will act in a way that appears contrary to the laws of physics. The ball will slow or stop completely and then change direction and accelerate uphill, make multiple right-angle turns and even stop completely and then rotate as if spun by an unseen hand. Often accompanying activity that is childlike are EVPs of a small girl calling "Mommy" and a woman calling "Carol." Carol's parents, Jack and Lucy Janney, were the last full-time residents at Kendrick House. Perhaps mother remains where her child passed away.

A different type of activity experienced at Kendrick House may be connected to fear of the violence of the Civil War. A black mass has been observed that cannot be adequately described as a shadow. It appears to have mass and as if made up of writhing strings or worms. Most often this black mass is encountered on the second-floor landing, sometimes hovering in midair as if a cloud. Its presence often coincides with a distinct heaviness in the air. This black mass takes interest in men but has not been known to interact with women or children unless engaged directly. During preparation for an investigation, the technical team was setting up equipment when the mass was observed. As a male tech was setting up a camera in an upper corner of the landing, he was facing the rear of the house. Meanwhile, I and other investigators were taking baseline readings of the electromagnetic fields (EMF) in and around the house. I and another investigator were standing in the backyard measuring EMF when my companion looked up and saw the black mass in the upper far corner of the landing. Upon further observation, the mass did appear to be made up of smaller dense objects that writhed about one another, and over the period of about thirty seconds, the mass itself began to take on a conical shape, with the narrow end of the cone pointed toward the back of the tech who was working on the camera. As we watched this transformation, the black mass seemed to start to move toward his back. I said reflexively in a low tone, "Leave him alone." As if in response to my words, the mass stopped in midair, changed direction and then accelerated quickly at me through the landing window. As it came through the glass, it no longer was visible, but a second later I felt an impact, as if a solid object flew into my chest and bounced off. It had enough force that I took a half step backward and caught my balance. The investigator who was with me stated that she felt pressure around her for an instant just as I stepped backward. Although something ran into me, I did not experience fear or feel threatened; it was more as if it was telling me to stay out of the way. Looking around us, our gaze returned to the landing window, and once again the black mass was hovering about the ceiling of the landing, and the tech continued working on the camera and cable unaware of its presence. The investigator with me went inside and up on the landing. As she waved her arms toward the ceiling, I observed the mass from where I had been standing. The mass was unaffected. Then a male investigator joined her, and as he waved his hands toward the ceiling, the mass shrank into a smaller ball in the upper corner. When the mass has been observed, often men present are touched or pushed in an uncomfortable manner. Additionally, two male investigators have experienced a time anomaly after encountering the mass and responding in aggressive or assertive tones with the mass. However, each perceived the anomaly differently. One investigator felt the atmosphere as oppressive and walked outside for air. He was absent for almost an hour but upon returning inside indicated he thought he had been outside only a few minutes. The other affected investigator became upset and went into another room alone. Within three or four minutes, other investigators joined him, but he was convinced he had been alone for several hours and that he had been unable to find the other investigators. Note that these negative experiences were correlated to an aggressive response to the black mass. Other male investigators have not shared that experience. This is a good illustration of the reason that I do not advocate the use of provocation during paranormal investigations.

At times, the black mass has appeared in a human shape, a featureless black mass but again with the internal movement of writhing string or worms. At the end of an investigation, we had packed up our equipment and carried it outside at about 2:00 a.m. Four of us returned inside to double-check that we had not left any equipment and to turn off the lights. We regrouped in the first-floor hallway to walk out when a loud thump was heard, as if someone stomped on the floor. Someone asked, "Was that outside?" and the other three of us replied by pointing up toward the ceiling. One of the investigators stepped to the foot of the staircase and looked up. The rest of us watched his face drain of color, his eyes widen and his mouth drop open. He shook his head no and walked past us muttering, "I'm out of here." I and another investigator went up the stairs looking for whatever had startled him while the third member followed him outside inquiring about what he had seen. Upstairs we found nothing—no mass, no heaviness in the air…nothing. Outside, we heard the description: a black squirmy mass in a general human form standing at the landing railing, slightly bent forward as if returning his gaze. He was most disturbed by the fact that the mass had blocked out the rocking chair on the landing that was directly behind where

The second-floor landing where a black mass has been observed leaning over the railing as if looking at the people at the bottom of the stairs.

it stood. As I listened to the details on the front lawn, I observed a shadow person stand up from behind the bushes planted along the front of the house and walk across the lawn to stand behind the ancient cedar tree west of the sidewalk. It seemed to stand still, partially visible in the moonlight behind the tree as we talked. I walked, circling the tree to get a better view, and the shadow person crouched low and then disappeared. This was a shadow person as typically seen and not the black mass.

While this human-shaped form of the mass is similar to the appearance of a shadow person, this is a different type of entity. Such "creatures" are found in voodoo and hoodoo lore. They are alleged to be the conjured manifestation of a spell meant to protect someone or something from harm. In early Missouri, voodoo and hoodoo was a common practice among slaves. We know that horrific violence befell at least two slaves at the Kendrick farm during the Civil War. Likewise, there would have been times when the men were absent, either serving in the Confederate army or for other reasons, leaving the slaves, women, children and elderly male family members alone. Since the black mass appears to be wary of certain men, and no women or children have been affected, it may be possible that the black mass is a bound, conjured manifestation of a spell to protect the women and children left vulnerable during the war. Interestingly, as Paranormal Science Lab has spent many hours at Kendrick House, the presence of the black mass is seen less frequently. Perhaps we are no longer seen as a threat.

Civil War Stories

Whispers Around the Campfire

I have spoken with a number of Civil War reenactors who say that paranormal experiences are not uncommon during reenactment activities. Stories are often related over campfires during battle reenactments. It is not surprising that these events would trigger activity. Even at this distant date, artifacts are still recovered on occasion, including musket balls and items intimate to the soldiers' experiences in life. The sights, sounds and smells are evocative of the real-life events that transpired some 150 years ago. Unexplained mists and intense smells of flavored tobacco (often vanilla) are typical reports.

Kendrick House is far from the only place evoking Civil War activity in the area. Many skirmishes were fought across southwest Missouri, and many are poorly documented. Much of the fighting on the Confederate side was waged by guerrillas, and small-scale clashes often were not recorded in detail. Apparitions of Civil War soldiers have been reported in places known to have had armed action, as well as places not as easily verified as having connections to empirical fact. There are oral accounts of hauntings at farms north of Carthage known to have been in the path of fighting during the Battle of Carthage and that were occupied at that time, including recollections going back generations in a family. I have heard stories of people hearing noises associated with troop movements, such as that of galloping horses when no horses are around or the sounds of men marching or running through underbrush in open, empty fields.

Left: Jesse James as he appeared at age sixteen when he was a Confederate guerrilla fighter operating in southwest Missouri.

Below: Many ghost sightings have been reported during Civil War reenactments and encampments in the area. Reenactment photo.

Nearby Avilla demonstrates activity associated with the chaos of guerrilla warfare. Although it had been founded for less than ten years when war broke out, Avilla was a Union stronghold, and Dr. Jaquillin Stemmons and his family illustrated the resistance to secession. Stemmons was representative of those slaveholders in the region who held fast to their loyalty to the Union and did not see owning slaves as a basis for rebellion. As war approached, Stemmons formed a military company for the Union. Stemmons freed his slaves, as he felt that was the best means of protecting them and ensuring their survival in the coming war. Most of those former slaves decided to stay with the Stemmons family despite their freeman status, and years later, several of the former slaves described Dr. Stemmons as a kind man and father figure whose surname they willingly took for their own. The Stemmons family ended up divided, with one of the doctor's sons fighting for the Confederacy. Dr. Stemmons was shot to death on March 8, 1862, by Confederate bushwhackers in a raid during which his home was also burned.

The attack on the Stemmons home was intended to intimidate the local Union men from opposing the Confederate cause in southwest Missouri. Instead, Avilla townsmen decided to approach the bushwhackers from an offensive posture rather than the defensive stance relied on up to that point. The citizens in Avilla took up arms. The Union army gained possession of Missouri in 1862, but the region remained overrun by bushwhackers and occasionally small bands of Confederate regulars or guerrilla raiders on horseback. It was estimated that at any given time, the area between Nevada (approximately sixty miles north of Carthage) and the Arkansas state line at the south end of McDonald County, Missouri, some fifty miles south of Carthage, would contain up to one thousand guerrillas and bushwhackers. The Avilla town militia became a prototype for the future county militias. The patrol areas were extended within eastern Jasper and western Lawrence Counties. Patrols of mounted militiamen were augmented by a few Union soldiers of the U.S. Cavalry from Fort Scott, Kansas, and continued to protect the town and countryside in local skirmishes. The militia gained a reputation for tracking down and shooting bushwhackers, who came to fear the Avilla pioneer marksmen.

By 1863, Avilla was a Union army garrison manned by the Enrolled Missouri Militia under the command of Major Morgan. Tents were erected, and storehouses, barns and homes were converted to temporary army barracks and headquarters that housed hundreds of soldiers at various times and a number of refugees. The town became known to the Missouri militiamen informally as "Camp Avilla," and by 1864, many of the original town militiamen continued to assist the new Missouri Militia functioning as patrol leaders in the newly organized Jasper County Militia. Avilla supported anti-guerrilla operations in the region while under Lieutenant Colonel T.T. Crittenden of the Missouri State Militia's Seventh Cavalry and functioned

One theory for the many sightings of Civil War soldiers in the area is from the fact that many were buried in unmarked graves.

as a way station when needed in the transportation of Confederate prisoners of war. Being situated in open grassland, Avilla was able to maintain a formidable and effective defense and became a sanctuary for refugees of nearby burned-out towns such as Carthage.

In one account, a Rebel's skeleton was found just south of town with a bullet hole in the skull; he was never identified. He had apparently been killed during a previous skirmish with militiamen, but his remains were not found until they were in an advanced state of decomposition. The skull was then hung from what became known as the "Death Tree" and remained suspended from a tree limb for over a year near the road at the Dunlap orchard, now abandoned and defunct, as a warning to all other bushwhackers. Some accounts have the tree being an Osage orange or hedge tree that appeared dead. Some accounts say the tree was an apple tree and then stopped producing fruit and that black crows took up a continual perch in the dead branches.

A ghost story has grown out of the Avilla Death Tree accounts. Referred to as the Avilla Specter or Avilla Phantom, it is said the bushwhacker whose head was displayed still wanders the fields surrounding Avilla. This phantasm is reputed to be aware or interested in the living who stray past and takes interest in scaring the unwary passersby. If true, this could be a different type of entity, perhaps the kind of ghost that returns to torment the living or a revenant, or some type of interactive or intelligent ghost, as it appears aware of what is happening and behaves in a manner that could be intended to frighten witnesses. Witnesses have described him as a lurking, headless shadowy figure in a long duster and an antique firearm slung on his back. The phantom bushwhacker sometimes stands with an outstretched hand as if searching for something, but he has also been seen crawling low to the ground, as if trying to avoid detection of militia patrols. The phantom is seen most often on cool autumn nights along the roads and fields surrounding Avilla. Some assume that he searches for his head or skull, which was disturbed and placed in the tree. Some have dubbed the frightful ghost Rotten Johnny Reb. Witnesses have claimed to have shined a flashlight on the ghost, and the beam "went through like he was transparent, before we ran away frantically." Legend has grown up that if you can find the old tree from which his skull hung, under certain light you may see the image of the skull and perhaps send the Death Tree Phantom to the other side. My first impression of the legend of finding the tree was that it would be nearly impossible, as it was common for a hanging tree to be cut down to avoid bad luck befalling the area. However, it may not have been viewed as a hanging tree, as the victim was not hanged but the skull later found and placed in the tree. There are very old trees in the area, so it is possible that the tree still stands.

Avilla today is a quiet hamlet along Highway 96 (old Route 66). There are abandoned commercial buildings as well as active businesses. Not much from the Civil War years remains, but the streets are laid out much as they were during the war. There are legends of various shadow people being seen along the main street and businesses. Shadow people are thought to be paranormal entities that appear as dark shadow forms in a general human shape; most appear featureless. Some have been said to appear in the old park just north of the highway, standing under abandoned store awnings, in windows and even walking through the locked doors of the U.S. Post Office (old Avilla Bank Building). These shadow people may be residual in nature, meaning that they are an imprint on the environment and replay events from the past. One of Avilla's shadow people has been called "Otis" by some, in reference to the town drunk character on *The Andy Griffith Show*, as it seems to stumble from the old tavern building that dates from the late 1860s and allegedly has been seen lying down on the road. Residual hauntings are theorized to occur due to extreme emotion experienced in a location, such as extreme elation, terror or sadness. The experience of the residents of the area during the Civil War certainly would involve the potential of imprinting emotion in this location, if imprinting is possible. While the old tavern and post office were not built at the time of the war, there were structures in these areas, so it may be possible that these shadow people are reliving events that occurred on the site but in different physical structures. Could it be that the drunken behavior observed of the shadow person called Otis could perhaps be of a man shot and stumbling out of a house or other structure and falling down, rather than passing out from intoxication?

There were many soldiers and civilians who were killed not in battle but by lynching or summary execution who seem related to later accounts of ghostly encounters. In the Reeds area east of Carthage, an injured, ill Union soldier was taken by guerrillas out of a farmhouse at which he was convalescing and was executed. The guerrillas rode off, leaving the body near a pond. The teenage girls of the house buried the soldier in an unmarked grave where he had fallen. Over time, feelings of being watched and feeling uncomfortable and odd noises around the pond led to stories that the pond was haunted, and people tended to avoid the pond, particularly at night.

A woman in the Reeds area related the following in the past two years. She was standing at her kitchen window washing dishes. The view out the window overlooked an open pasture. She looked up and saw a man walking through the pasture toward her direction. She watched to see who this was coming across her land, and as he neared, she clearly made out a Civil War uniform. The witness stated that it was a bright, sunny day and that the soldier was fully formed with a shimmering appearance. He seemed to

The Avilla Post Office, originally the Avilla Bank, is built on the site of Civil War–era structures, and shadow people have been reported walking through its locked doors.

The Norris girls wait for the Federal troops to march through downtown Carthage to unfurl the Stars and Stripes hidden in petticoats. Reenactment photo.

Many of the skirmishes in the area were fast moving, and records were not always well kept. Casualties could not always be accounted for, leading to situations where the fallen were not buried or given a proper burial. Reenactment photo.

Above: A lone Civil War soldier is seen crossing a field and takes notice of the witness. Reenactment photo.

Left: Belle Starr learned the skills she later used as the "Bandit Queen" as a Confederate spy during the Civil War as a teenager. Vintage print.

notice her watching her and raised his hand and waved with a smile. He continued walking, and as she continued to stare after him, he disappeared. The apparition has not been seen again. She was confused as to why a Civil War soldier would be in that field. The answer may be lost to history, as so many small clashes occurred in the area without being recorded in detail.

Civil War events may also explain, at least in part, activity observed over time in Central Park on Garrison Avenue. The tranquility of this green space may be deceiving. This is actually the site of the first city cemetery and was the resting place of many early settlers, as well as casualties of the Battle of Carthage. Once a national cemetery was established in Springfield, Missouri, the graves of the soldiers were reinterred in the national cemetery. Later, the land was turned into Central Park, and the remaining bodies were moved to other local cemeteries. Decades later, during improvements to the park, it was discovered that some of the bodies had not been moved, although no grave markers remained. Sightings of apparitions in period clothing have been made in the park area over the years. While there is often speculation as to haunted cemeteries, my personal experience has been that cemeteries are not haunted per se, but a haunting may be a result of improper burial or other events on the site such as a death. In this case, it is likely that disturbed graves or removal of the burial markers have contributed to ghostly activity.

Battle of Carthage Park

Eternal Reconnoiter

What is now a historic site and park off River Street was native prairie with a fresh spring and sharply rising hill, ideal for observing anyone approaching the camp in 1861. On the top of the hill sat the James House, site of an Underground Railroad stop, which reputedly also utilized a cave by the spring. The Union forces camped here the night before the battle. It was also the site of the last several hours of intense fighting of the Battle of Carthage. As the Federal troops retreated toward Sarcoxie to the east, the Confederate troops set up camp here. There would have been troops on picket, and in particular, they would have been quite interested in the movements of the Federal troops, as well as the civilians in the area.

The manicured grass, perimeter of trees and pool of water give the impression of a peaceful expanse, which can easily lull one into a sense of being alone. However, it would seem that soldiers are still on watch in this quiet place, although it is not obvious at first glance. There is a well-worn footpath that ascends the hill, traverses the spine of the crest and comes back down the other side, winding through thick trees and brush. It is on this slope that a soldier with a slightly transparent appearance has been caught peering from behind trees.

During investigations by Paranormal Science Lab, the soldiers on sentry appear to have come even closer in the main part of the park that would have contained the encampment. Over time, an area on the west side of the park produced frequent interesting data. Consistent EVPs were obtained of a man urgently calling out to a "Webb" and warning of danger. Very

Entrance to the Battle of Carthage Historic Site and Park.

Entrance to the grounds of the Carter House, which overlooks James Spring and the Battle of Carthage Park.

interestingly, results varied depending on the composition of the team of investigators. When a group of female investigators was in that area, audible footsteps would be heard circling the women, so close that the sound of swishing trousers would also be heard. When women only were present, EVPs focused on warning of danger. However, when male investigators were present, EVPs were more guarded and the auditory sounds of footsteps were less frequent. The impression left was that the entities present were more cautious of the male investigators. This seems consistent with Civil War–era soldiers who would be unsure of whether men present were friend or foe but protective of women. Additionally, it was common for women to act as spies and couriers for the troops operating in the region.

I had a more unusual experience in the park at the end of an investigation, as I and the other team members were walking through the park toward the parking lot. I happened to be at the rear of the group as we walked. It was a clear evening, but suddenly the air around me had the sensation of weight.

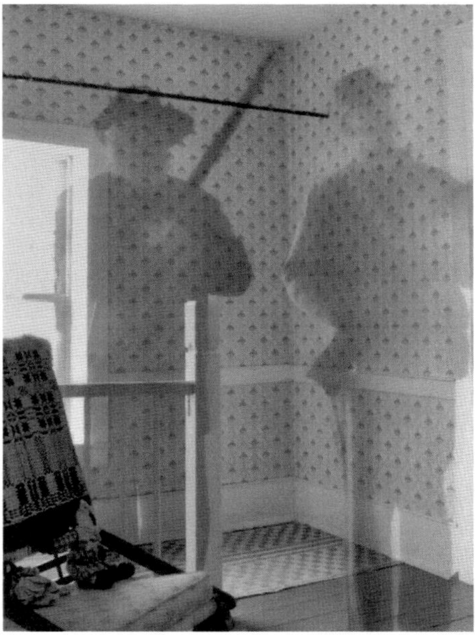

Left: Often, women and children were unwilling witnesses to violence and destruction. Many lost their homes to the scorched-earth policies employed by both sides and were forced to leave the area. Reenactment photo.

Right: Images of ghostly soldiers are a frequent paranormal experience. One has to be careful to analyze evidence of ghosts. This photo was produced with specific photographic techniques to achieve the effect. Reenactment photo. *Courtesy of Alex Martin.*

It felt as if a heavy blanket had been thrown over me. I called out to the others ahead of me, but no one heard me. I felt restrained, as if fighting my way through a barrier. After the others had traveled about twenty yards, I was able to step forward, out of the heavy area. I took a gulping breath, feeling as if I had run out of air, and called out again. This time, the others immediately turned at hearing my voice. I looked back over my shoulder and was surprised to see a shadow person that seemed to be in the outline of a man in Civil War uniform, holding a musket. I have not had this kind of sensation before or since that day. I have heard of this type of experience, but I have no rational explanation for it.

Shadow forms have been observed by others moving through the park without an explanation. Another investigator relayed a firsthand experience to me. He was standing in the park when he felt someone put a hand on his shoulder. He turned, expecting to see one of his companions. Instead, he saw an apparition that had detail. He could make out a slouch hat and a duster. The entity had a rifle in one hand, with the barrel resting against his shoulder. The apparition pulled his hand back, turned and started walking and then faded away. The witness's sense was he had seen a guerrilla fighter. It certainly is possible that guerrilla units camped at this spring at various times during the war. Another investigator related a different encounter with a shadow person in the park. She was taking pictures with a digital camera while with two other people. A picture was taken, and while waiting for the image to appear on the viewfinder, the screen, normally white, was filled with a dark silhouette in the shape of a person from the head to the chest. It disappeared in an instant, but three people present who were looking at the camera waiting for the image of the photograph to appear observed the silhouette. When more pictures were quickly taken, the silhouette was not present. It was described as filling the viewfinder, as if a person was standing directly in front of the camera.

It appears that the ghosts in the park are still on picket, guarding the camp. As they scrutinize visitors for potential threats, they boldly make themselves known. While it is likely that this activity is connected with the Battle of Carthage, the landscape makes this a defensive stronghold, and it would have been a likely campsite for regular troops and guerrilla fighters alike as the war wore on.

HAUNTED DOWNTOWN

POSTWAR GROWTH

The end of the Civil War signaled the resumption of building and business in Carthage. All but a handful of prewar structures had been destroyed. The town quickly resumed its prominence as a commercial center. Below is a firsthand account of Carthage in the last half of the nineteenth century that gives context to ghost stories that have grown up in the intervening years:

> Carthage Press
> *January 19, 1949*
> *76 Years a Carthaginian*
>
> *R.D. Jennison—Richard Daniel Jennison has been a resident of Jasper County since his birth something over 77 years ago, has been a resident of Carthage 76 years, worked in the mines in the northwest part of town when Carthage was an important ore producer and has been a continuous subscriber to the* Press *for 58 years and a reader of this paper for 68 years. Mr. Jennison thinks—and this should shock the Chamber of Commerce—that around 1892 before the "Cleveland depression" Carthage was a better business town to the square inch than it is now. "People argue with me about this," he says, "but there must have been well over 10,000 people here then and it certainly was a busy, bustling and prosperous place."*

The late 1800s brought renewed prosperity to Carthage. Vintage image, circa 1890s.

BORN NEAR LARUSSELL

Mr. Jennison was born September 20, 1871, in a two-story log house on a 240-acre farm about the present site of Larussell, the son of Mr. and Mrs. D.A. Jennison. The father, Massachusetts-born and a union veteran of the Civil War, had come to Carthage overland in a covered wagon with a party of colonists from Wisconsin in 1868 and for awhile had engaged in the shoe business here—then moved to the farm. In 1872 when the son was about a year old he moved back to Carthage and re-entered the shoe business, being partners with a Mr. Woodmansee on the east side of the square. They made shoes to order in those days as well as selling custom-built ones. The family house was on the west side of Fulton Street just south of Central and there were not so many trees and houses in that part of town then. From their back yard they could see plainly the Jasper County jail which had been erected in 1872. Mr. Jennison well remembers the public hanging of John Ables in 1878 which he saw—or nearly saw—from his back yard. The family gathered in the back yard to watch proceedings over at the jail. With them were some of the neighbors for whom this was a better viewpoint. They could see the erected scaffold and the condemned man led on to it. That was enough for 7 year-old Dick Jennison. He looked away. That sort of thing might, as people said, have a salutary effect on youth but he didn't want to see it. "You know," says Mr. Jennison, "everyone seems to think that

that scaffold was on the west side of the jail where later executions took place. Looking back in memory it seems to me that it was on the east side. Of course I was a child and my memory on that may be at fault."

BAPTIST CHURCH SCHOOL

He first went to school in the old Baptist church on the corner of Maple and Central—went there his first two years. The only other school building in Carthage was what was later known as the Central, where the high school [present-day junior high school] *now stands, and since it could not take care of everyone the school board had rented the church for weekday use. Then the Washington school was built on Fulton Street south of Chestnut a block, and he went there. He attended Sunday school at the Methodist church where the Drake Hotel now stands. R.H. Rose local merchant, was superintendent, he recalls. Later the Franklin school on Maple street north of Miller street was built and he attended there, his father having in the meanwhile moved to the corner of Thirteenth and Clinton streets. His teacher there at first was Miss Kate Fisher, later the late Byron Ash. Finally he went to the Central school which had high school classes on the third floor. Sometime in the early eighties the Missouri Pacific railway was built right through town on Parsons street and the boy watched the grading and track laying on this, the more interested because he had heard his father tell when the first railway train came into Carthage July 4, 1872, on what is now the Frisco line, he had gone to Pierce City to come in with it. It was quite impressive to him that building of the Missouri Pacific down Parsons street. D.A. Jennison was a friend of I.N. Lamb, who owned a lot of ground at the northwest edge of town and was prospecting for mineral there. Mr. Lamb told him if that he struck ore he would give him the first chance to buy a mining lot—an acre—on which to sink a mine of his own. Mr. Lamb struck ore and his friend, in partnership with Aaron Myers became a mine operator. The 18 year-old son went to work at the mines, first driving a horse-hoister as a shaft was sunk, then later working at various jobs about the mines as machinery and mills were installed.*

MUCH MINING HERE THEN

"This was just west of Parsons street south of Limestone," says Mr. Jennison. "It was rich ground and a number of mines were in operation. There were seven mills inside the limits then. Soon ore was found on the Lindsey mines just southwest of town, and later the Pleasant Valley still farther south opened up. Carthage stood high in the list of producers in

The mining industry brought fortune to many in business in Carthage, enabling them to build fine Victorian homes.

The Victorian homes of Carthage represent varying architectural styles.

those days. Sometimes as much as a trainload of ore went out from those mines in the northwest part of town alone—mostly zinc but some lead." "Those were the days when Carthage was really booming. In addition to the mines there were a lot of industries—the flour mills, two woolen mills, the foundry on Oak and Garrison, a big canning factory, a couple of brick plants, eight quarries as I remember and a lot of other things. There was a big pottery, for instance, north of Limestone Street. Carthage was going strong in those days. It is now too, of course, but those seem to have been the really big days to me." Joseph Crowley, a union veteran of the Civil War like Mr. Jennison's father, came down from Vernon County to work for Mr. Jennison in the mines. Dick Jennison heard that there was a daughter in the family and thought that it might be well to cultivate her acquaintance. He did. He and Miss Agnes Crowley were married here December 13, 1891. They celebrated their golden wedding anniversary December 13, 1941, and are looking forward to their sixtieth anniversary.

DEPRESSION OF 1893

In 1893 came the great depression which people, according to their habit of blaming things on the man in the White House, called "the Cleveland depression." The wheels of industry stopped. The price of ore dropped to virtually nothing. The mines closed down. "People say it was the water that closed those mines," says Mr. Jennison. "It wasn't. It was the depression. Of course when efforts were made to re-open the mines there was water and it was hard to beat. I tried mining out there again myself. But it was the depression that shut down that field." Thereafter Mr. Jennison worked at various occupations, mined occasionally, farmed some, did some market gardening. One of his last mining activities was as a superintendent of the Main Street Mining company, belonging to J.W. Ground and W.R. Logan. This mine was south of Fairview and east of the present water tower. "I operated that mine myself awhile after Mr. Ground and Mr. Logan quit," recalls Mr. Jennison, "doing some work that they would not let me do while I was working for them. I did pretty well at it too—made over $300 a week for awhile, I remember. No, I wasn't pulling the pillars. That ground was left sound and it hasn't ever caved in. What I did was to take out the floor separating an upper level from a lower one. That was the rich ground." Later he went into the fuel and timber business—stove wood, cord wood, railway ties. He sold about 2,800 ricks of wood a year to Carthaginians then. He furnished 4-foot wood for the Coahuila mines northwest of Carthage to burn under their boilers during a coal strike. The *last year he was in this business he furnished 2,000 railway ties for the quarry switches. Mr. and Mrs. Jennison now live on West Mound Street just north of the Boggess & Graul addition. Rev. Herbert Jennison of Carthage is a son. One daughter, Lola May, died in infancy, Miss Neva Jennison died in 1931 and Luther Estle Jennison died in 1937.*

Tribute to Wife

Mr. Jennison is laudably proud of his wife. "When I lost a part of my hand in a buzz saw," he says, "she did a lot of work around the place I couldn't. For instance—she cultivated 40 acres of corn. I suspect that not many women have done that. A few years ago I took her to a ball game. She did not want to go very much because she did not think she would be interested. But now she goes to more ball games than I do. She has not missed one at Municipal Park here during the last two years and has attended a few out-of-town games as well." It is the old days in Carthage that Mr. Jennison is prone to talk most. Circuses used to show in Carthage on College hill north of Central and east of Fulton streets—P.T. Barnum and others. Like most other old residents Mr. Jennison is not sure why it was called College hill. He supposed there had been a school there before the war and when he was a boy there were the ruins of some brick buildings on the hill. A.M. Drake, hardware man, William Motherspaw, livery stable man, and J.M. Whitsett, dry goods man, were friends and sympathetic with the desire of boys to attend circuses. Boys soon learned that if they dropped around Motherspaw's livery stable then on Grant street at a certain time on circus day that the three likely would take them to the circus.

He's a Fair Man, Too

Fairs have always interested Mr. Jennison. He and Mrs. Jennison have attended every one held in Carthage since their marriage. First there was the one south of Fairview avenue east of the Missouri Pacific railway. Mr. Jennison helped set the posts for that. Then there was the Knell fair that became the Jasper County fair. "Incidentally, it is about time that fair was revived," says Mr. Jennison. "It seems to me that young Frank and Bob Knell would be good ones to do it. They could get a lot of good counsel from their aunt, Miss Emma Knell." Then there were the balloon ascensions. Carthage merchants used to stage them on the square on Saturdays before the court house was built, they serving to attract trade. Bill Easton, who lived at the Grant Street hotel on Sixth and Grant used to be the balloonist. Mr. Jennison believes that Mr. Easton broke in Fred Ambrose, who later became noted in that line. He likes to recall the old businesses in Carthage. He believes that there has always been a hardware store on the north side of the square where the Carthage Hardware Company is now located—at least there has always been one there in his memory. Jesse Thacker ran it first as he recalls it. "That is a statue of Jesse Thacker out in Park Cemetery just west of Baker Boulevard near the end of Cedar Street," says Mr. Jennison. "Looks just like him too as I recall him." A clerk there named Henderson was once Mr. Jennison's Sunday school teacher when he was a boy. Later Mr. Henderson bought into the store and it ran as Henderson & Huntley. Still later the store became Keim-McMillan—H.M. Keim and Joseph M.McMillan. Then it became the Carthage Hardware store operated by C.C. Carter for many years.

"Really a Town in 1892"

He likes to recall the old parks. Wildwood Park on the west side of Spring river just south of Tucker's ford northwest of Carthage was once a famous one, patronized not only by Carthage people but people from nearby towns. This was a favorite place for boating and picnicking. Just east of the river was a half mile track, a very busy place on Saturday afternoons and Sundays, Mr. Jennison recalls, though in his recollection there was more foot-racing there than horse-racing. But he likes especially to recall the days

This aerial view facing south over the Carthage square illustrates how the city was rebuilt and expanded. Vintage postcard.

> *of 1892, the year before the big panic hit. "Carthage was really a busy place then," he says. "They tell me it is better now but that isn't according to my recollections. She was really a town back in 1892."*

Many of the postwar structures are standing today, and they have their own ghost tales. On the north side of the square, on the site of John Shirley's hotel and tavern, sit Carthage Hardware and an antiques store. There are stories of paranormal activity in these buildings, with sounds of unseen patrons. To the west of the square is the original Knell Mortuary building, which has housed multiple businesses over the years. The building still has evidence of the horse stable in the basement, and people have reported hearing footsteps when no one else was in the building.

Above: The original Knell Mortuary building.

Left: The balloon launches were not the only extravagant activities in Carthage; here a man is captured racing down this towering ramp on a bicycle.

On the south side of the square, one building was originally a bakery from the 1880s onward for a number of years. I have heard firsthand accounts of people seeing a man in white work clothes, including an apron, in the building. He is described as wearing a handlebar mustache but having a slightly transparent appearance. The man walks through the building, often in early morning hours, as if still in the midst of his work.

At 418 Grant Street, just off the southeast corner of the square, is McMorrow's Triple L Bar building. This building has been retail and/or warehouse space since being built around the turn of the twentieth century. At times, there have been apartments upstairs as well. Unexplained events have occurred here over time. I spoke with one witness who described events on a Sunday evening. While walking on Grant Street, a man in a suit was observed standing on the sidewalk in front of McMorrow's. The man walked into the building, and the witness did not take special note until realizing that it was Sunday evening, and therefore, the bar would not be open. Approaching the door, the witness looked into a dark building with no sign of anyone inside. Shaking the door, it was confirmed to be locked. The witness stated that it was a matter of seconds from when the man walked in the building and his reaching the door. The witness was convinced that no one was inside.

Upon being contacted to conduct an investigation of the building, Paranormal Science Lab toured the building and interviewed more witnesses. Employees recounted seeing shadow movement and items being inexplicably moved, such as glassware. There were also testimonials of seeing apparitions in the building. The multiple accounts indicated that there may be a woman and a man present.

There was reported paranormal activity throughout the building. Sounds of glass clinking near the bar and what sounded like the front glass door opening and closing were overheard by multiple investigators. EVPs of a man's voice were also documented. While walking through a hallway, the question was posed, "Where are you?" and in reply, a man's voice was recorded saying, "Right behind." At this time, the identity of the man who seems to remain in the building is unknown.

Proceeding east to the corner of Fourth Street and Howard, one comes to the Drake Hotel. Construction began in 1920, and it opened for business in 1922. It was not the first hotel in Carthage, but it was touted as modern and designed to cater to businessmen and well-to-do travelers, with fine appointments such as the ornate marble lobby and staircase.

It also featured a fine restaurant. Staff lived in the building as well. Over the years, much joy and sadness was experienced in these walls. The

McMorrow's Triple L Building, where an apparition of a man has been seen walking through the locked door.

Interior of McMorrow's Triple L. The sound of clinking glasses and other noises normally heard in a busy bar can be heard, despite its being closed.

The Drake Hotel.

tragic story of Celia Brennan is illustrative of the emotions that may have contributed to later ghostly encounters. Celia was only twenty-two years old when she was working as a waitress and living at the Drake Hotel. An illegal abortion led to infection. Despite being taken to the hospital, the infection became septic, and she died on June 28, 1935.

Over time, whispered stories of unusual events took hold. Feelings of being watched, the sensation of footsteps on a bare floor and other hints of not being alone became more common. The building fell out of favor as a hotel over ensuing decades. It went through hard times, but in recent years, it has been renovated to its former glory and is an apartment building. Even with the remodeling and improvements, I have heard people describe the unsettling feeling of being watched and sensing that unseen presences are with them. Perhaps some of the former residents linger in this elegant building.

One can see Jim's Bar from the sidewalk in front of the Drake Hotel. The employees and patrons of Jim's Bar have not hidden the fact that paranormal activity occurs in this one-hundred-year-old brick building. Reports include shadow movement that is not explained, and on occasion, disembodied voices can be heard. The source of the activity is unclear at this time.

Jim's Bar has been the site of unexplained paranormal activity over the years.

This has been the site of the Jasper County Jail since the 1870s and witnessed executions on the grounds.

The west side of the Carthage square. The Carthage Kress Department Store was the first Kress store west of the Mississippi. Vintage photo.

At the intersection of Fourth Street and Lincoln stand two buildings with interesting connections. There are many very old houses in the area, and there have been reports of seeing apparitions in windows and other unusual events. On the southeast corner of the intersection stands the Jasper County Jail on basically the same site as the previous jail, built in 1872. Aside from countless people who have passed through the cells here, executions were carried out on this site from the 1870s to the 1930s. Directly across the street is the William Rozelle Logan House.

Logan Landmark

Family Fortune and Tragedy

William Rozelle Logan ran the Carthage Stone Company, among other mining interests in the Carthage area. Carthage Stone was the first company to quarry Carthage limestone on the land owned by the Kendrick family. That quarry is still in operation. William married Julia Sennett and set up house at 403 West Fourth Street in Carthage. The two-story wood-frame house was pure Victorian in details. As the 1890s saw Logan's contemporaries building extravagant brick and stone homes on Grand and Garrison Avenues, Logan fought fire with fire and added a story to the house—on the bottom. The original house was raised and the current first floor was added, including its ornate Carthage marble façade and wraparound porch. This is the reason why there appears to be a formal entrance on the second floor, as that used to be the front entrance to the house.

The Logans were the picture of the American dream. Business prospered and life looked enchanted from the outside. What surely was a happy household seems to have fallen under a dark cloud as the family suffered unexpected illness and death. On September 8, 1923, Julia died suddenly at the age of sixty-two from a cerebral embolism. William next buried his son William Rose Logan, who died unexpectedly on January 27, 1932, at the age of thirty-six from heart failure and kidney disease. William next buried another son, Frank Logan, age fifty-five, who passed away from cancer on October 3, 1938. William Rozelle passed away less than a month later on October 30, 1938, of a cerebral hemorrhage at the age of

The William Rozelle Logan House at 403 West Fourth Street.

The Phelps House, one of the beautiful examples of Victorian homes on Garrision Street.

eighty. William's other son Mac continued to reside in the house with his wife, Jennie. Jennie then died of a cerebral hemorrhage at age sixty-eight on January 28, 1951. There were at least these five deaths of the family members living in the house.

The house passed out of the Logan family, continuing as a private residence for many years. It has long had a reputation of being haunted. Perhaps the fact that it is situated across from the jail lends to the legend, but stories of ghosts persisted over time. Paranormal Science Lab investigated the house after it had sat empty for several years. The empty rooms and dilapidated condition of the house cast a pallor over the interior. Dirt was thick on the floors, and the rich woodwork and architectural accents were dull. Parts of the house were open to the elements, and animals had invaded the top floor.

Despite being vacant, the house had a definite heavy atmosphere, and feelings of foreboding were experienced by the investigators. The chandelier hanging over the staircase landing would be found swinging as if pushed when no one was near the staircase. However, the fixture was out of reach when standing on the landing, and the swinging movement was not reproduced when attempted through jumping, stomping feet, etc.

Almost a universal reaction while in the house was that of being watched by a hostile presence and at times the sensation of not being able to breathe. The weather was cool, and no atmospheric factors were identified that would create those sensations. No remarkable auditory evidence was captured, but several team members reported seeing two shadow people on the first floor. While shadow people often avoid direct contact with the living, these shadow people stood fast, almost as if challenging the intruders to leave. It was also noted that being in the house seemed to negatively affect one's mood.

The conclusion reached was that there is likely paranormal activity occurring in this house. It seems most likely that activity is connected to the manner of passing of the Logan family members. These were sudden deaths, and theories abound that sudden deaths can leave a spirit unaware of the fact that it has died. Under these theories, a spirit will often be very attached to a place and/or belongings that had deep meaning in life. Perhaps if this is the case in the Logan House, the family members lingering view the living as intruders or are still experiencing the sense of panic and fear of the moment of their death. Are these emotions being communicated through energy manifested by the culmination of those unpleasant feelings? Were we feeling the anxiety and confusion experienced by the Logan family members who died sudden deaths? Were members of the Logan family attempting to keep

Above: When more opulent homes of William Logan's contemporaries were being built on Garrison Avenue and elsewhere in Carthage, he simply had his house lifted and a new first floor added.

Left: Unnamed Victorian lady, taken by a Carthage photographer in her home. Vintage photo.

us at bay to keep the house to themselves? While no conclusive evidence was found as to the nature of the paranormal activity, there is an indication that it is interactive and possibly confrontational.

It is not unusual for an entity to continue to be present in a home to which it was attached in life. Another example is at a house that is only a few blocks away from the Logan House. The house dates to the 1800s, but it appears from records that it was not the first building on the site. What is known is that there were at least two brothers who died in the house. It has been confirmed that one brother's name was Frank, and he died on January 18, 1934. The other brother, Charles, died on August 24, 1935. Frank's wife lived in the house for a number of years after the brothers passed away and had a passion for growing flowers. She spent much of her time tending her plants and flowers in a greenhouse on the property, as well as in the basement.

It is the brothers who have made their presence known. EVP sessions have indicated that Frank is present. However, responses also indicate that two separate men are in the house, and it is thought that Charles is this second male presence. Charles appears most often in the rear stairwell on the second floor. Originally in this area was a bathroom as well. Frank makes his presence known upstairs in the area of the bedrooms. He has been seen standing, as if watching over the current occupants. In the basement, shadow movement has been observed. No natural explanation for the shadows was identified, and one has to wonder if Frank's wife is still tending her flowers and plants. The presence in the home is not angry or fearful, as at the Logan House. Perhaps the difference in energies is related to the emotions felt at the time of death.

Nighttime Visitors

The Watchers

A phenomenon that is fairly common but can be very unsettling is an entity sometimes referred to as a "watcher." Typically, firsthand accounts describe a full-bodied apparition appearing in a bedroom and standing silently while the occupant of the room is sleeping. In some instances, the apparition is seen walking into the room, even through a solid wall. Occasionally, the witness sees the entity come into the room before he goes to sleep, and when he wakes, the entity is still standing watch and then walks out.

The first local example was at a house in the southern part of Carthage. The house was built in 1914 and has a more modern addition to the rear. Fortunately, I was able to hear the experiences of not only the current owners but the previous owners as well. The previous owners, a married couple, both experienced watchers. Both stated that they would awake during the night to find an elderly couple, man and woman, standing at the foot of their bed silently. Their descriptions of the man and woman were consistent with each other, and it is assumed from the details that they were seeing the same entities, although they did not necessarily both see the entities at the same time in each instance. They related that they were not frightened or upset by the presences but felt calm.

The current owners relate slightly different experiences. The husband has not witnessed activity, but the wife and three teenage children have each had experiences. The eldest daughter has witnessed multiple apparitions standing in her bedroom doorway and in the adjoining hallway. In particular, a young

Stately homes were an expression of the prosperity in the area.

man made an impression on her. He was wearing contemporary clothing and was covered in dirt, loose grass and leaves, as if he had been rolling on the ground. His appearance may reflect the manner of his death. No death in the immediate vicinity is known to involve facts that would have resulted in this appearance, although the possibility exists.

Auditory events are also present in the house. An example was related by the wife. She was in her bedroom off the front living room during midday. She was alone in the house, and she heard the front door open and then close. The family dog reacted by running to the front of the house and barking aggressively. Then heavy footsteps were heard walking across the floor, and the dog stopped barking and started jumping as if playing with someone. Thinking that her husband had come home for lunch, she called out, but there was no reply. She walked into the front room to find the dog sitting, wagging her tail, looking excited as if she was anticipating being petted. This incident may be related to a watcher as well, since the feeling was that the dog was familiar with whatever was in the room, was not threatened by it and seemed to be interacting in an excited manner. Perhaps whatever made the sounds of the door opening and closing plus the footsteps is an entity present in the home often, and the dog is comfortable with the entity. This would be consistent with a watcher who is present on a regular basis. There may be a scientific explanation for pets acting as if they are aware of unseen presences. Dogs and cats see further into the light spectrum than humans, and as energy phenomena, paranormal entities may be visible at frequencies outside the human range of vision. The same is true of noises. Dogs and cats also hear sound at frequencies not audible to the human ear.

Since watchers tend to not speak, communication does not seem to be a primary goal or function. Instead, they appear to be standing guard or watching over the living as they sleep. Often, watchers are described as being in a child's room. They may be a protective spirit to ensure no harm comes to the person during slumber. However, not all entities who watch appear comforting.

The next experience occurred at a home in Carthage dating to the 1800s that has been in the same family for multiple generations. Two family members told me their experiences, which were independent of each other, occurring decades apart. Both described an entity that watches at night in the bedrooms. Both described feelings of foreboding and fear when the entity was present. The younger witness described the entity as animal-like but moving on two legs. The older witness also described seeing an entity watch while she would lie in bed. She said it would sit on its haunches and had the appearance of a gargoyle or animal with leathery-looking skin and no hair. Both felt that the entity did not appear as a human apparition. Both seemed affected, discussing the subject as if the experiences were still very vivid. The entity did not speak or communicate, as typical of watcher

Italianate design was also featured in a number of homes.

experiences. There is no known historical event at this location to explain the fearful emotions evoked in these experiences or the non-human appearance of the apparition.

The last example most closely approximates the prototypical watcher experience. It occurred at a house in south Carthage built in the 1960s. No record of tragedy or death was found as happening in that location. Living in the home are a married couple and their seven-year-old son. The boy, referred to here as Andy, began talking about a man in his room when he was a toddler. His parents at first assumed he was describing an imaginary friend and did not think much of his morning stories. Over time, it became obvious that he was interacting with something in his room, sometimes speaking to an unseen person, pausing in intervals and then responding to unheard statements or questions.

Andy began giving details of the man's description, including the gray suit he wore, eyeglasses, build, etc. The man would walk into the room through a wall as night fell and Andy prepared to go to bed. He would walk over toward the closet and stand in front of the closet door and watch Andy. Andy would go to sleep with the man standing watch. When Andy would wake in the morning, the man would be standing in the same spot and then silently turn and walk out of the room through a wall.

Shortly before our investigation, Andy was looking at family photos with his mother and surprised her when he pointed to a picture of her grandfather, who died while she was pregnant with Andy. Andy smiled and said, "That's the man who comes to my room." Andy's mother was startled but not surprised that her grandfather would be watching over Andy. EVPs indicated that a Charles was present. Andy's mother confirmed that her grandfather's name was Charles and that he went by Charles, not Charlie or another familiar name. Most often, watchers appear to be a spirit with a close connection to the family and more often than not seem to be protective of children.

Prosperity School Bed and Breakfast

Ghostly Lessons

Prosperity began as a lead and zinc mining camp west of Carthage. The Troup Mining Company was opened in 1888 and was located on forty acres of land that eventually became known as Prosperity. Among its main investors was Curtis Wright, a furniture maker from Connersville, Indiana. Apparently, he set out to Missouri in order to seek a new challenge. Wright was also an amateur geologist and came to the Joplin mining district to indulge that interest. He liked what he saw and wrote home, promising his wife that if she would agree to the move, he would build her the biggest house in Carthage. He added that he planned to invest in the lead and zinc mines but intended to make his new career in the limestone quarries of the area. True to his word, Curtis Wright built a magnificent Queen Anne–style home for his wife, Nira, and also became involved in the limestone industry, operating the Carthage Stone Company and other related companies. His home, formerly located at 304 West Macon, was built in 1891 and constructed of local limestone and timber. Wright placed rock from his mines on the façades of the eaves.

So began Prosperity, Missouri, located at the end of a branch of the Southwest Missouri Electric Railroad and on a spur of the Missouri Pacific Railroad. By 1899, more than twenty mines were in operation, and a population of over 1,500 made Prosperity much more than a mining camp. In 1907, Tom Tarrant and his brothers built the Prosperity School from local Carthage stone and red and yellow bricks to serve the swelling numbers of families with children. Like most schools of the time period, it served all

The Prosperity School Bed and Breakfast.

grades. During its heyday, Prosperity had a bank, stores and other businesses. The Joplin area mining district experienced a decline with dropping lead prices during the late 1920s. There was an increase in demand during World War II and then the final decline after the war as cheaper sources were developed overseas. This marked the beginning of the migration from the town of Prosperity. The school held on and operated until 1962, when it had about 30 students left. Now all that remains of the once-prosperous town is the school building and a few homes.

After the school closed down, the building stood empty for more than thirty years until the current owners, Richard and Janet Roberts, purchased it in 1994 and renovated the building, keeping the architecture very much the same as when it functioned as a schoolhouse. The building reopened as the Prosperity School Bed and Breakfast in 2000. The school gained a reputation over the years as being haunted, and often, teenagers would enter it in the dead of night. Rumors of it being haunted continued even after the building became a bed-and-breakfast. I have spoken to people who attended Prosperity School as children, and some are very hostile to the notion that the building is haunted, feeling that it gives the school a negative image. On the other hand, its reputation for being haunted has drawn visitors to stay the night. However, from the perspective of a paranormal investigator, it raises the issue of how the stories of paranormal activity originated. Having grown up within a few miles of the Prosperity School, I can say I have heard stories since my childhood of it being a scary place that some people considered haunted, but many abandoned buildings hold that reputation. I had not heard detailed firsthand accounts that would give these stories authenticity, so I was unsure if these stories were merely made up by teenagers who had scared themselves in an empty building. Additionally, it has become a destination for paranormal investigators, including The Atlantic Paranormal Society (TAPS) of the television show *Ghost Hunters*. Video footage of what are claimed to be the ghosts of young children running down a hall has appeared on the Internet. The video was impressive on first viewing, but it is hard to judge from the camera angle whether these shadows could be cast by people running down the hallway, as the camera was in a cross hallway and only a narrow field of vision can be seen in the video footage. Needless to say, I was definitely curious to find out for myself when PSL had the opportunity to conduct an investigation at the Prosperity School Bed and Breakfast.

The inn is a wonderful mix of the former school and a lovely bed-and-breakfast. It is very nicely decorated and homey, yet it retains the charm of a schoolhouse, including the coatroom next to the restrooms, the former stage incorporated into one of the guest suites and the original bell tower above. Four members of PSL arrived on a sunny afternoon to meet the owners and conduct an initial walkthrough of the inn. The Robertses are gracious and enjoyable hosts. The inn displays many items documenting the school's past, providing many potential "trigger objects"—items that may have meaning to any ghosts or entities in a location that could be a source for paranormal activity.

The current dining room and the parlor directly beside it are separated by a large archway. These rooms are said to have paranormal activity, including the sounds of school desks and chairs being scooted across the floor and footsteps, perhaps from students or maybe a janitor cleaning at the end of the day. The centerpiece of the dining room is a large, ornate dark walnut dining table with a glossy finish. We were shown small fingerprints on the table that, on inspection, are set in the finish, as if children touched the surface while the lacquer was still damp. The owners attest that the fingerprints were not always present. According to the Robertses, they were seated around the table one evening with a paranormal investigator they are acquainted with, and when they got up to investigate something they heard, they returned to find the fingerprints there. They attempted to wipe the prints off with polish but to no avail.

It was at this point in PSL's tour that a shadow person revealed itself. A shadow person does not cast shadows on the floor or wall as a living person or other solid object. While we were in the dining room and parlor area talking with the Robertses, I happened to be standing in the corner of the dining room, diagonal from the door to the main hallway. As I was standing there, contemplating whether the fingerprints were made when the finish was still wet, I watched a shadow person come to the doorway, lean forward as if looking into the room very quickly and then rush past the open doorway. It was a bright, sunny day, and the hallway was well lit. Everyone was in the dining room and parlor, so no living person could have caused the shadow. It was approximately four feet tall. Unfortunately, since we were on an initial walkthrough, no cameras were set up. However, my observation of the shadow figure indicated that there was a chance that paranormal activity could be documented there. Our investigation occurred on a warm early summer night with clear skies and no breeze. The area is rural at this point, with very little noise contamination from the road or surrounding area.

One story that is circulated as a possible cause for any haunting at the Prosperity School Bed and Breakfast is a tale of a teacher and mother of a student arguing upstairs. As the story goes, during the confrontation, the little girl was somehow accidentally bumped into, and she lost her balance and fell out of a second-story window. This story has not been confirmed as true. Another ghost story involves an antique cabinet with doors and shelves sitting in an upstairs hall leading to one of the suites. The owners state that guests have reported a nurse dressed in an early twentieth-century uniform standing in front of the cabinet, hand extended, as if picking up bottles or jars off shelves and looking at them. Now the cabinet is full of linens and towels, but the cabinet was found in the basement of the building, so it is possible that it was a supply closet for the school nurse at some point in time.

Three of the four guest suites are named for longtime teachers at the school. Miss Pink Saxton's Room is decorated in shades of pink and burgundy and has an antique brass bed with a private bath featuring a claw-foot tub with a handheld showerhead. Miss Rose Saxton's Room is cast in shades of green and has a four-poster canopy bed and plenty of roses. Miss Pansy Smith's Room features a high-back Victorian bed, a New Orleans armoire and walls covered in pansies snuggled amidst amethyst tones. The Prosperity Suite rounds out the choice of suites with an elegant high-back bed and matching décor.

Rose's room is the site of multiple phenomena. Guests have been awakened by the sensation of a small child crawling into the bed beside them, even feeling tugs on the blankets. One woman who was staying in the room by herself said that she was awakened by this sensation but, in her drowsiness, thought it was one of her children and fell back to sleep, only to awaken the next morning to the realization that it could not have been one of her children as they were not with her. Rose's room is also known to play havoc with electronic equipment, including cameras. We experienced this situation with our cameras during our investigation. Three cameras were set up, recording to a digital video recorder. On multiple occasions during the investigation, an area of distortion would appear on the video, almost like heat radiating off hot asphalt during the summer. However, the area of distortion would move about the room. If an investigator was in the room when the distortion appeared, the distortion tended to move toward the person and appeared to distort the image of the person as if something with mass was situated between the person and the camera. We attempted to find a natural explanation for this distortion but without result. There were no strong EMF fields, unusual lighting or other conditions identified that could have affected the quality of the video. The cameras were changed out with other cameras to verify that the cameras had not developed a malfunction, but the replacements experienced the same distortion. We were informed by the owners that similar activity had been observed by other paranormal investigators.

Pansy's room includes a Jacuzzi-style bathtub. We were informed that, on occasion, the motor that runs the water jets will turn on by itself and run. The owners said that this started not long after it was installed, and the manufacturer has attempted to find the cause for this apparent defect but found the tub in perfect working order. Likewise, no defect in the wiring was found. The cause for this unusual activity is unexplained. The bathtub remained silent while we were present.

At the end of the second floor, near the staircase, is an open area where an antique table sits under a window. The owners informed us that one evening during an EVP session around that table, questions were being asked about any Civil War activity on the grounds. An EVP was captured naming a doctor. After some research, Mrs. Roberts said she was able to confirm that there was a doctor so named who served in the Civil War and was part of a unit from Indiana. While this may seem a mere coincidence, it cannot be dismissed without further review. A number of units from other states, including Indiana, fought within the state of Missouri. While it has not been confirmed that this doctor was in the Prosperity area during the Civil War, it is possible, as records of units were far from complete, especially here in the western theater. One seemingly mundane fact contributed to incomplete unit records: the scarcity of paper needed to write the reports. In truth, there may well have been a skirmish on the grounds surrounding Prosperity School, as southwest Missouri saw some of the most intense guerrilla warfare in the Civil War.

Pink's room was the center of activity during our investigation. Cold spots with temperature drops documented by thermometers were detected and could not be explained by any draft or air conditioning. EVP sessions were conducted multiple times during the night with surprisingly consistent responses. These responses indicated that the spirit of a woman who was a teacher at the school was present. During some of the EVP sessions, multiple flashlights were used as objects for an entity to interact with investigators. Questions were asked, requesting that the entity turn on a light if the response was yes and not turn on a light if the response was no. In other sessions, questions were asked, requesting that the entity turn on a blue flashlight if the response was yes and turn on a red flashlight if the response was no. The responses using both methods were consistent. The responses indicated that the teacher, Rose Saxton, was present and that she was not sad or lonely.

While sitting on the bottom stair, an EVP session was conducted that produced two interesting EVPs of a male voice. The first EVP was about forty-five seconds into the session. After asking if anyone there liked the owners, the audio recorder captured an EVP of a man's voice replying, "In charge." About twenty-five seconds later, an investigator asked the question, "Where are you at?" and the same voice replied, "Right behind."

We set up cameras in three directions, trying to duplicate the video showing shadows of children running down the hallway upstairs. We placed them at both ends of the hallway facing each other and also placed a camera in the intersecting hallway in the same position as the camera in the video. Unfortunately, no anomalies were captured in the hallway. As such, no conclusion can be made about the video of the running shadows. The video does make an impression, but without seeing video from the ends of the hallway, there is no way of objectively evaluating the cause of the shadows.

There do appear to be anomalies present at the Prosperity School Bed and Breakfast. Are there former students running the halls, teachers still leading classes or other employees such as a nurse or janitor going about their routines as they did in life? Could there be Civil War soldiers or perhaps miners who died in the immediate area also occupying space within the old schoolhouse? I know I saw a shadow move down the hallway in broad daylight without a satisfactory explanation, although we could not count the experience as evidence since it was not captured on camera. EVPs and strange distortions that moved around in the camera frame were captured. There does appear to be paranormal activity, but the exact nature is yet to be determined. Regardless, a night in the Prosperity School Bed and Breakfast, whether as a paranormal investigator or a guest, will leave memories unlikely to fade quickly.

JASPER COUNTY COURTHOUSE

THE PAST REFUSES TO FADE AWAY

The Jasper County Courthouse on the square in Carthage is built on the site of the two-story brick courthouse that was destroyed and burned in the Civil War. After the war, the site was cleared, and the center of the square remained open and empty until 1893, when construction was begun on the present courthouse. It is reputed that a workman died from a fall in the clock tower area during construction. Another worker is reputed to have died in a fall while installing the elevator. There have been public executions on the courthouse lawn as well. There have been stories of ghostly activity in the courthouse over the years, as well as of apparitions on the courthouse lawn, including what appear to be Civil War soldiers. If there were to be ghosts of soldiers in Carthage, this is a likely place with the intense fighting, destruction and death that happened on this very ground.

The present courthouse is a massive building of limestone, Carthage marble, built more in the style of a fortress than a civic building. Perhaps the comparison was intentional—a testament to the aspirations of those who rebuilt Carthage into a thriving commercial center and perhaps as a triumph over the days of burning and depredations during the war years, a building for the ages that will not be consumed by fire. Countless dramas have played out within these walls over the ensuing 114 years, determining the fate of those involved. Members of Paranormal Science Lab had the privilege of being the only paranormal investigators given access to the courthouse.

Employees have had various experiences in the building over the years that cannot be explained by natural or man-made causes. The attic area and

The Jasper County Courthouse at night.

clock tower have been long-rumored to be the site of a haunting. These areas are not accessible by the public, and the clock tower is closed off. PSL was given access to the attic area, and full-spectrum cameras were set up with audio recorders. On camera, there were a couple of instances of shadow movement that was unexplained and was not reproduced by experiments. Anomalous audio evidence was obtained, with the sound of footsteps when no one was in the attic.

The majority of other reported activity centered on the third floor, which is occupied by courtrooms and offices related to the court. A very interesting story comes from a former bailiff who worked in the courthouse for many years. He was a skeptic by nature. However, one morning shortly before Christmas, his wife brought in cookies for the court personnel. They walked into one of the original courtrooms to place a plate of cookies on the desk and were confronted by a disembodied voice: "What are you doing there?" They both reacted to the voice and, after setting the plate down, left without replying. They were positive they were alone in the courtroom and the voice did not come from another area. They were left with the conclusion that they experienced something out of the ordinary. The towers and turrets on

The imposing presence of the courthouse offers a sense of why the preceding courthouse was viewed as a highly strategic advantage position by both sides during the Civil War.

the perimeter of the building are functional, housing offices and restrooms. The women's restroom on the southwest corner of the third floor has its own ghostly presence. A shadow person has been observed walking through this room and reported by employees.

Due to the sheer size of the building, cameras and audio were concentrated in the attic and third floor. Battery drain was a recurring problem, causing interruptions in filming and audio recording as well as other battery-operated equipment such as EMF detectors. This anomaly is common in locations experiencing paranormal activity, and it is theorized that entities draw energy from batteries to interact or manifest. Additionally, the cameras were not functioning in the women's restroom, and after changing out cameras and cables multiple times, filming had to be discontinued in that room. In the courtroom in which the audible voice was heard, EVP sessions resulted in audio capturing a soft male voice stating he had stood trial there. It appears that there is anomalous activity in the courthouse. However, the identity of the entity has not been ascertained.

HAUNTED SCHOOLS AND HOSPITALS

PAST AND PRESENT

One of the most haunted sites in Carthage exists in memory alone. Fairview Acres opened as the Jasper County Alms Home, commonly referred to as a poor farm. People who were unable to care for themselves were given a place to live. Later, it was turned into a nursing home. The massive stone building was eventually torn down, and the Family Y now sits on the site. The old stone guardhouse is the only remaining evidence of the imposing facility. For years, stories of ghostly apparitions and unexplained noises filtered out. Firsthand accounts center on auditory evidence. People would be heard going about daily routines unseen. Feelings of uneasiness were common as well.

The offices of the city's Public Works Department are housed in the original McCune-Brooks Hospital. However, McCune-Brooks was not the first hospital on this site. City Hospital sat in the general area of the present parking lot but was torn down when McCune-Brooks opened. McCune-Brooks was renowned for paranormal activity. Over time, parts of the upper floor were closed off and left unused. I have been told firsthand accounts of former staff members who said that going to the top floor was an eye-opening experience. Witnesses tell of sounds of gurneys rolling through dark, abandoned hallways. The most startling was the story of seeing white nurse's shoes walking across the floor. One witness told me she heard these stories from older employees and was very skeptical. However, when challenged to see for herself, she headed upstairs with other employees who swore they had seen these things personally. She told me she was amazed when she in fact

The City Hospital sat where the parking lot of the original McCune-Brooks Hospital now sits. Vintage postcard.

The original McCune-Brooks Hospital has long been the site of paranormal activity.

saw what looked like feet and lower legs wearing white nurse's shoes walking in the empty space. It was as if the apparition started materializing from the feet up and went only to the calves.

Likewise, many today would be surprised to know that the white brick apartment building sitting at the corner of Garrison and Twelfth Streets was also a hospital. It was Memorial Stone Hospital, the doctor-of-osteopathy hospital in the days before doctors with a DO degree were allowed privileges

Many would be surprised to know that this unassuming apartment building is the former Stone Memorial Hospital.

at McCune-Brooks. People who have lived in the building have reported unusual occurrences. Reports of paranormal activity seem most concentrated on the second floor in the area of the morgue, now part of an apartment. Reports focus on unexplained noises, voices and shadow movement.

Perhaps one of the more unusual tales of paranormal activity in Carthage is associated with the old high school. The auditorium is reputed to be haunted, and the apparition of a young woman has been seen in the area outside the auditorium. The source of the haunting is not specifically known.

Burlingame & Chaffee Opera House

Cannons, Theater and Murder?

The Burlingame & Chaffee Opera House building stands at 136 West Fourth Street, on the southeast side of the square in Carthage. The building is not the first structure at that location. In 1861, at the beginning of the Civil War, two buildings stood on the footprint of the current building: the mercantile house of J. Robertson, the first brick storehouse in Carthage; and a saloon operated by a Mr. Pennington. These structures were obliterated during the repeated burnings and battles in Carthage. After the war, the downtown area was slowly rebuilt. In 1877–78, the current building was constructed. Francis Chaffee had been engaged in the hardware business in Carthage with Robert Howell for some years. Chaffee undertook the construction of the building with W.L. Burlingame and conducted his business on the first floor of the building. Paranormal activity was reported by construction workers; they complained that while working in the excavated area that would become the basement of the opera house building, the distinct sound of cannon fire was heard.

The Burlingame & Chaffee Opera House, housed on the second floor of the building, debuted on February 21, 1878, with a ball attended by approximately two hundred people, with music provided by the Carthage Light Guard Orchestra, an adjunct of the Carthage Light Guard Band, part of the local militia. The *Carthage Banner* described the second-floor opera house:

The Burlingame & Chaffee Opera House building is the current home of McBride's Antiques. The building to the left was owned by John McCrillis, who operated McCrillis Hardware in the Burlingame & Chaffee building.

> *The hall is 53 by 100 feet with an 18-foot ceiling. The stage is at the north end and is 20 feet wide. There are two well-arranged dressing rooms at either end of the stage. Two private boxes overlook the stage and house. The comfortable seating capacity is 640 and, without crowding, 800 people can be seated. It is furnished with very comfortable opera chairs throughout. For acoustic qualities, the hall has no equal in the West.*

The opera house hosted traveling theatrical troupes as well as amateur performances. It was well appointed, including sets designed and painted by artists and commissioned by the owners. The opera house also served the community in addition to being an entertainment venue for the well-to-do citizens. The *Carthage Evening Press* reported, "The ball given at the opera house on Christmas Eve [1878] for the poor of the city was fairly well attended. The music was good and peace and harmony prevailed throughout. In due time, supper was announced and all repaired to the St. Charles Hotel where a beautiful meal was waiting, prepared expressly for the occasion."

The west side of the Burlingame & Chaffee Opera House building is adorned with a mural celebrating the opera house's role in the community.

Robert Howell passed away, and John D. McCrillis purchased Howell's share of the hardware business downstairs. Chaffee retired several years later, and McCrillis's brother Frank joined him in the hardware business, although Burlingame and Chaffee continued to own the building. The opera house was used for many years as a meeting hall as well as an opera house, and graduation ceremonies for Carthage High School were conducted there for a number of years. The opera house space was leased to Jasper County during 1893–94 for use as the courthouse while the current courthouse was being constructed.

In 1898, John D. McCrillis set in motion a series of events that may be contributing to the haunting experienced in the building today. McCrillis found love letters from his good friend and neighbor William Gilfillan, president of Gilfillan Stone Company, written to McCrillis's wife. John McCrillis must have had a tortured night, because the following morning he walked to the Gilfillan house and invited his old friend to breakfast. After eating, the two ended up on the square in McCrillis's hardware store, where McCrillis pulled out a revolver and shot Gilfillan. Gilfillan ran outside and collapsed in the street at the corner. A belief has pervaded that McCrillis was never tried for the murder. However, the law did not ignore the situation, although the outcome may be hard to reconcile:

> Adams County Union Republican, *Jan 5, 1899.*
> *A JUSTICE HOLDS GILFILLAN'S SLAYER WITHOUT BAIL.*
> *Carthage, Mo, Dec. 31* [1898]—
>
> *The arguments in the preliminary hearing of John D. McCrillis charged with the murder of W.J. Gilfillan were completed at 6 o'clock last night and at 10 o'clock this morning Justice Garland rendered his decision, holding the defendant without bail.*
>
> *Attorney Gray created something of a sensation by charging the justice with having been imposed upon by letting himself be taken to the home of Mrs. Gilfillan, widow of the dead man, for the signing of her testimony. "The attorney for the prosecution was there" said he "but neither I nor John McCrillis knew anything about it. But I do not blame you. They took advantage of your age and condition."*
>
> *The eye of the venerable justice filled with tears as he said: "I had no intent of doing anything wrong. I only went there to save her from having to come down town again. It was at my suggestion it was done and I take all of the blame."*
>
> *Rising from his seat the justice turned to McCrillis and said: "John, I have tried to do my duty in this matter," to which McCrillis replied with a firm voice. "It is all right, uncle Tommy. I have no complaint to offer."*

Perhaps empathy for the circumstances in which McCrillis found himself contributed to the acquittal, a silent condemnation for the dead man. The *Los Angeles Herald* reported:

> *THE MCCRILLIS MURDER*
> *NOW ON TRIAL AT CARTHAGE...CARTHAGE, Mo., Dec. 27.—The criminal court room was packed this morning at the trial of John D. McCrillis, accused of the murder of W.J. Gilfillan. Many strangers were present, attracted by the knowledge of the prominence of the parties. The taking of testimony was delayed until 10:30, as the lawyers for the defense were delayed by reason of belated trains. The first witness was Miss Lula Powers, who was employed in the McCrillis family for some months. She testified that the deceased, W.J. Gilfillan, was in the habit of making*

frequent visits to the house during the time that Mr. McCrillis was away from the city; that the deceased was not accompanied by his wife. These visits were often at night and continued until after she had retired to rest.

On cross-examination she said that Mrs. Gilfillan was also a frequent visitor, as were the children; that the families were seemingly very friendly. When asked to recall whether these visits dated back to the first day of her entering the family as a helper, she could not state positively, but said they did occur four times daily.

Dr. L.I. Matthews, formerly of Carthage, but now of Joplin, was the attending physician in 1896 and 1897. He remembered Mrs. McCrillis' condition at that time. She was suffering from nervous prostration; remembered her going west for her health. In her state of health she was easily influenced. The state in cross-examination wished to know if sending Mrs. McCrillis across the continent unattended, without the comfort of a sleeping car and confining her expenses to 825 per month and without the care of a husband, would not influence her mind. This was objected to by the defense, as it was altogether false and nothing had been introduced indicating that it was probable. Some time was consumed in arguing this point, and court adjourned.

Ultimately, McCrillis was released on $15,000 bail, an extraordinary amount of money in 1899. Although he would not be found guilty in a criminal court, Mrs. Gilfillan did not let the matter lie. An interesting side note is that Mrs. Cora Sennett Gilfillan was the sister of Mrs. Julia Sennett Logan, whose own family tragedy played out in the Logan Landmark House. Cora Gilfillan sued McCrillis in a civil suit for $5,000 in economic damages suffered as a result of the death of her husband. The widow prevailed at trial, and McCrillis, not content to pay the judgment, appealed, arguing that the murder was justified due to his learning that the dead man had been having an affair with his wife. McCrillis's argument was rejected, and Cora's lawsuit still stands as good precedent for the proposition that such circumstances do not constitute a valid defense to economic damages resulting from killing a person.

In 1905, Chaffee sold the Burlingame & Chaffee Opera House building to the C.E. Turner Harness & Carriage Co. for $25,000. The building was occupied by Turner Harness & Carriage as well as the Carthage Furniture & Carpet Company. The Turner family conducted a successful business in the building for a number of years, ultimately as the Turner Furniture Company. Later, it was occupied by the Burr Variety Store until the Turners

The south side of the square, circa 1910. The Burlingame & Chaffee Opera House building was then owned and operated by Turner Harness Carriage & Furniture Company. Vintage postcard.

sold the building to the Belk-Simpson Department Store chain in 1958. Belk's operated a department store in the building until the late 1980s, followed by Bee's Variety Store.

After sitting empty for a time, the building found new life in the twenty-first century. A couple from California purchased the building with the intent of remodeling it and living on the top floor and running a business downstairs. A work crew was employed, and the couple stayed in the building as they worked. Framing and sheetrock went up on the top floor in the rear of the building in anticipation of an apartment. Renovations were begun elsewhere in the building, and over time, the couple ended up sleeping on all three floors of the building after the work crew would leave for the night. Before long, they noticed strange things occurring around them, which to begin with were dismissed as imagination or caused by fatigue. Footsteps were heard in various parts of the building in the silence of darkness, as were noises that could not be explained, other than to say it was an old building. The activity escalated and culminated on a late night when they were sleeping in a basement office put in by the Belk Department Store. Around 3:00 a.m., they were awakened by a wall-shattering noise. In the darkness, the husband grabbed a gun he kept for protection and ran up the stairs, expecting to find that a car had driven through the front of the building. He found the building intact and just as they had left it upon retiring to the basement. It had sounded like an explosion or cannon fire. By 8:00 a.m., they were packed and driving back to California, never to step foot in the building again. When showing the building to the current owner, the husband handed over the keys and lingered on the sidewalk. The current owner, Keith McBride, thought that detail was unusual but did not put much thought into it as he toured the building. It was only after purchasing the building and having his own experiences that the former owner's reluctance to enter the building began to have meaning.

McBride had previously operated his antiques store in another building on the Carthage square, and he was preoccupied by moving the business into the Burlingame & Chaffee building, as well as various repairs. However, as a daily routine settled in, odd things became noticeable. On virtually a daily basis, heavy footsteps would be heard upstairs, as if someone in work boots was walking across the floor. The only outside access is by a staircase that has its own entrance to the side of the building. Although the door was kept locked at all times, initially, McBride would hurry upstairs to see who was up there. Each time, he would be confronted by empty space. As time

This mural is just north of the square and features advertising for the opera house and the Carthage Light Guard Band, which often performed at the opera house.

went on and more events occurred without realistic explanations, he had the added complication that employees and customers began discussing their own unexplained experiences. McBride brought in Paranormal Science Lab to document the paranormal activity and rule out man-made or natural causes.

Hearing footsteps is the most common reported unexplained activity, including the sensation that the footsteps are following you around the store. The sound of furniture or heavy objects being moved overhead has been reported on the main floor as well. These reports are not confined to employees and customers. A contractor who was upstairs to make an estimate on some contemplated work came downstairs and, with a nervous expression, confided, "You do know the building is haunted, right?"

In the old opera house, auditory phenomena are most common. In addition to footsteps, EVPs of operatic singing have been documented, as well as several distinct voices. A woman's voice is captured on audio most often, seeming to be trying to call attention to herself, saying things such as, "Over here." A woman's scream has also been captured on video, accompanying a visible distortion in the air near one of the old dressing rooms. There is lore that there was a shooting in the theater area while it was being used as the courthouse, but it is unclear from sources whether the shooting actually occurred in the court at the opera house or at another site used as a courtroom at various times between the time the previous courthouse was destroyed in 1862 during battle and the completion of the current courthouse in 1894. Other sounds occurring in the area include what seems to be an old-time cash register ringing and the drawer opening, followed by the jingle of coins falling into a drawer. This occurs in the area where the cashier's box was located in the opera house. Employees who have had to go upstairs to attend to heating and air systems have been caught off guard by the phantom cash register ringing up ticket sales. There is no cash register upstairs, and the cashier's box is partially dismantled.

The area that seems to have the biggest impact on visitors is the back stairwell and adjoining hallway, where people report a foreboding feeling. EMF spikes are common in this area despite the fact that there is no live electricity in that part of the building. On one occasion, while preparing for an investigation, four PSL team members were upstairs setting up a camera and audio recorders. As the group went down the back stairs to the main floor, they stopped on the landing in response to a clearly heard voice of a young girl calling urgently, "Wait!" The voice was as clear as if someone were standing a few feet away, and all four investigators reacted by stopping and turning toward the voice.

The stage and office area at the front of the opera house is the site of the most visually compelling evidence of paranormal activity on this floor. A black mass has been captured on high-speed video at 480 fps (frames per second), which is approximately sixteen times faster than real time (30 fps) and double the maximum speed at which the human eye can detect movement (240 fps). It was captured in the area where the stage originally stood. It appeared as an upright column with a rounded top without a human shape. However, it was detected moving in and out of frame on the video. It was not visible to the naked eye of those present. Another occurrence is the solitary man who stands at the westernmost window appearing to watch the street below. This is the area of the cashier's box and safe. He was captured in a photo from the rear and to the right. His silhouette appears to be of a tall man wearing a suit with his head lowered as if looking at the street below. His head is more transparent than his body, but upon close inspection, the folds of the sheer curtain at the window can be seen through his torso as well as through his head. In attempting to re-create the image, an investigator stood in the same location wearing a suit. By aligning his position with the photo of the apparition, it was determined that the apparition was of a man of about six feet, three inches, with very broad shoulders. The stand-in stood in slightly different positions and in some frames moved his head as if captured in the act of looking downward out the window and moving his whole body in others, attempting to replicate the transparent appearance. In others, the curtain was draped behind him to attempt to create the appearance of the folds in the curtain. None of the re-creations approximated the original closely enough to satisfy reviewers, including impartial consultants. Who is the man standing watch over the opera house? It is unclear at this time.

On the main floor, now occupied by the antiques store, other presences have made themselves known. An area toward the rear of the building and close to the rear stairwell has been called creepy and described as having a heavy presence in the air. However, this floor appears to be the domain of an elderly woman and a small boy. Employees and customers have reported the feeling of being watched and thought they were followed about the store. A playful presence of a small boy is encountered in the store, most often in a storage room that in days past was a dressing room for the department stores in the building. Sounds of a child playing are

This page: These images were captured in the opera house. Note the image of a man standing before the left-hand window in the image below. No one was in that part of the building.

overheard, most often the sound of a popgun being fired. When the noise is investigated, it stops.

The boy is not alone and appears to be watched over by a grandmotherly entity. For example, in another storage room, while working alone an employee heard what sounded like three coughs. At first, he assumed he had

This image was taken with a stand-in for the apparition in the original photo.

heard a noise from elsewhere in the building, only to be corrected by the disembodied voice of an elderly woman saying, "Excuse me." He noted that the storage room was unusually cold despite it being a hot, humid day, and the storage room was not air conditioned. This is consistent with many reports of paranormal activity.

On another occasion, as the store was being closed, an employee was walking out but forgot his drink and walked toward the back of the store to retrieve the cup when he heard the voice of an elderly woman say, "Where is that boy?" The voice continued in an urgent voice, "Stop running!" The witness believed the latter statement was directed at him because he went through a very cold spot at that moment. A cold sensation seemed to seize his chest, causing him to stumble and clutch at his heart. As he came back to the front of the store, he relayed to McBride that there was an old woman back there, and at that moment his cellphone, which had been turned off, got extremely hot and burned him through his pocket. He took the phone out and tossed it at McBride, who confirmed that it was too hot to hold in your hand. This was a profound experience that left the employee with the feeling that he had come upon a conversation between two entities. He felt that he had stumbled into them and that the voice of the elderly woman saying "Stop running!" was meant as a warning to him to avoid walking through her and whoever she was talking with. He felt as if he had intruded on the entities, who meant no harm to him.

At the rear of the store, there is a wall separating the store space from the back stairs. Another experience in this area is the sound of a person falling down the stairs. This occurs almost every day at approximately 3:00 p.m. It is unknown if anyone ever died falling down those stairs, although while the Turner Harness & Carriage Co. and later the Turner Furniture

Company operated in the building, the upstairs was factory space, and finished products were either carried downstairs or brought down in a freight elevator. Also in this area, the sound of old-time piano music has been heard, apparently emanating from the basement. This may be due to the fact that one of the buildings on site that was destroyed in the Civil War was a saloon. Additionally, while the opera house was in operation, there was a saloon in the basement of the building on the east side of the opera house building. John D. McCrillis owned the building on the east side, and there were pass-throughs between the basements. It was common practice for the wealthy patrons of the opera house to partake of the saloon next door and then walk through the basement of the opera house building and ascend the back stairs to the opera house.

Activity in the basement is distinct from the rest of the building. Events from the Civil War appear to have imprinted on the environment here. As noted earlier, the sound of cannon fire was reported by construction workers while the building was being erected. Likewise, the previous owners experienced what they described as cannon fire or an explosion of some sort. During investigations, members of Paranormal Science Lab have heard the sound of black powder musket fire in the basement, and on occasion, the sound of musket fire has been followed by that of a woman crying. During recent remodeling, work was being done in the vicinity of one of the basement pass-throughs, and while one worker was facing the wall, a thunderous noise was heard. Fearing that a gas line had exploded, the witness ran up the stairs. Out of his peripheral vision, the lights in the basement were seen pulsating, as if affected by a shockwave. The building on the east side of the opera house recently burned down, but a former owner of that building has described hearing what sounded like cannon fire coming from the basement of the opera house building while he was in his own basement.

Not only are EVPs captured in the basement, but audible disembodied voices are also not uncommon in this area. People working in the building have reported hearing voices, including a couple seemingly in the middle of a domestic conversation. A man's voice was heard clearly saying, "It's a shame what the Huns are doing to our boys." In response, a woman's voice is heard, "Don't worry about it, and eat your supper." It is unclear if this is referring to Civil War events; although the term "Hun" was in use at that time, the term "Dutch" was commonly used in this area to describe German American Union soldiers. Another voice that has been heard by multiple people appears to be that of an African American man with a speech pattern indicative of the 1800s. An example of experience with this entity is that of an employee who walked into a room in the basement and started moving items stored there. A loud voice called out, "Wha' yo doin' there?" The voice has also been heard calling out to people in the basement, saying things such as, "Who's there?"

Apparitions have also been reported by multiple people in the basement. The girl discussed earlier seems to make appearances here, both heard as a disembodied voice, often calling out, "Mama?" and as a full-bodied apparition. She has been seen walking through the basement, usually toward the front of the building, and has been described as appearing about eight to ten years of age with blonde hair and wearing a white dress. Interestingly, an apparition of apparently the same girl has been seen in other buildings around the square as well. The identity of this girl is unknown, but one hypothesis connects her to the underground tunnels and caverns in the area. It is reported that there used to be entrances to the tunnels through basements in some of the downtown buildings. I have heard stories from elderly residents of children long ago exploring the tunnels. One story includes a tale of children becoming lost and dying in the tunnels. These oral legends have not been verified to satisfaction. However, it is my experience as a paranormal researcher that entities are not bound to a single spot or building, so this spirit may be traveling the tunnels from building to building for whatever reason known only to her at this point. Also seen toward the front of the basement is a light sphere, an internally lit ball of light that floats through the air and has been seen to pass through the wall at the front of the building.

The most vivid apparition described is that of a Victorian-era couple in elegant attire. They have appeared fully formed and as dense as living persons, startling a man working in the basement. At the time, the area was blocked off to the public for remodeling. As he worked, the man looked up and watched the couple walk into the basement on the east side, as if they had walked through the wall. He was dressed in a gray suit, and she was dressed in a white evening dress. Thinking that customers from upstairs had wandered downstairs, he called out, "Hey, no one is supposed to be down here." He approached them as they continued to walk toward the other side of the basement. As he neared and reached out to touch the man's arm, the couple disappeared. The worker was so startled that he ran upstairs and left the building, not to return until several days later. Who are the man and woman seen in the basement? It can only be speculated as of now whether they are a couple replaying a night at the opera or another event they are compelled to reenact over time.

On June 1, 2013, the building on the east side of the Burlingame & Chaffee Opera House burned to the ground.

Did the fire stir up activity connected to the burning of the buildings originally on site during the Civil War? Time will tell.

The Burlingame & Chaffee Opera House building has been resilient, outliving its contemporary buildings on either side. Most recently, the building on the east side, once owned by John McCrillis, burned to the ground on June 1, 2013. Amazingly, there was no fire damage to the opera house building, as if it is protected. In the hours and days following the fire, paranormal activity escalated throughout the building and, in particular, in the basement. Inconsolable sobbing of a child was audibly heard and would go on for up to a minute at a time. Shadow people were seen moving in the basement and running up the stairs, as if escaping danger. Bits of conversation were overheard, as if two men were in deep discussion but just out of range to be understood. EVPs of the girl were captured calling for her mother, as well as a woman asking for an investigator who was present by name. A man's voice was also captured in conversation with the girl. Also captured on video was a potentially interactive phenomenon. Three investigators were in the basement, and unexplained EMF spikes were documented. While holding an EMF meter, an investigator asked, "Can you tell us what is happening to you?" The question was immediately followed by an EMF spike, and on video, a white mist was captured coming into the frame in an elongated stream. The mist floated toward the EMF meter in the investigator's hand as the meter registered the spike, floated around the EMF meter and then floated out of frame in the opposite direction from which it had emerged.

What does seem clear is that the past refuses to be forgotten in Carthage. We never know when or where we will encounter the paranormal. Often, our lives intersect with a time past when it is the furthest from our mind. However, in certain places the barrier between the present and past becomes thin, and it is left to us to interpret the glimpses we stumble across.

Paranormal Investigation Methods

Paranormal Science Lab approaches paranormal investigations from an objective point of view. It is not assumed that unexplained events are paranormal in nature. Alternative causes are explored, and only if no other reasonable explanation can be found will anomalies be considered paranormal in nature. All investigations are documented by videographic, photographic, audio and other methods. Various types of data are collected during investigations, including atmospheric conditions, temperature, air pressure, static and fluctuating electromagnetic field readings. Data is recorded and preserved in electronic files.

Experiments are conducted during EVP sessions where PSL members conduct conversations or ask questions. High-end audio recorders, which are often used by musicians, are used to capture EVPs in the form of disembodied voices, as well as other audio anomalies that are not audible at the time of investigation. Tools employed include various models of ordinary flashlights. They are adjusted so that the battery connection is almost complete but also where the light is not on. The flashlights are placed on the floor, a table or other furniture. The floor is slapped with force to ensure that vibration from investigators' casual movement is not sufficient to cause the flashlight to come on. As questions are asked, any entities that may be present are requested to turn one or more lights on for an affirmative response and to leave them unlit for a negative response. Questions are asked in multiple ways for internal consistency; multiple responses are required, both affirmative and negative. PSL does not consider responses as an interactive exchange without consistent responses over an extended period of time (usually a minimum of a half hour) and with consistent responses on multiple flashlights of multiple models. An example of such sessions is on the PSL website at the investigations page for Kendrick House. Consistent responses involving as many as five flashlights at a time have been documented over as many as seven consecutive hours.

PSL also conducts experiments on kinetic energy, exploring theories of entities using available energy generated in the environment that is not electrical in nature. Children's balls of varying sizes, weights and materials are used and set in motion during EVP sessions, while the floors are

This is an example of an object that is the focal point of paranormal activity. This silver communion set was purchased by McBride's Antiques from a woman who had purchased it because it was inscribed to a church in Lamar, Missouri, from a couple in Connecticut in 1873, but she experienced poltergeist activity in her home once it was brought home. Once in the store, activity occurred that seemed to center on the communion set. EMF fluctuations were recorded around the set on all three floors of the building. Fittingly, through the author the set was purchased by John Zaffis and is now housed in the Zaffis Paranormal Museum in Connecticut.

measured for uphill and downhill slopes to determine if movement occurs that cannot be explained by the physical features of the floor and room. Colored stickers are applied to the ball so that movement can be observed more easily on video.

PSL uses multiple types of cameras, including wide-spectrum cameras (commonly referred to as full-spectrum cameras), which are sensitive not only to visible light, as are standard cameras, but also infrared light (utilized in night vision and security cameras) and ultraviolet light. This allows PSL to record portions of the light spectrum not visible to the human eye or standard cameras. Another type of camera used is a high-speed camera, which can record video at up to 1000 fps (frames per second). The accepted standard for recording real-time video is 30 fps, meaning that video at 1000 fps contains 33.33 as many frames as video recorded at 30 fps. The typical television program is replayed at 24 fps, slightly slower than real time. The human eye can perceive up to approximately 240 fps. This means that any movement faster than 240 fps will not be seen by the naked eye. When replaying high-speed video, the display rate is 30 fps, meaning that it takes 33.33 seconds to replay every second recorded. Every ten seconds recorded will take 333.3 seconds (five minutes and 33.3 seconds) to play back. The video will appear to the eye as being in slow motion but, in fact, captures movement that cannot be caught on standard cameras. PSL has captured movement appearing in a general human form that was not visible to the naked eye of investigators present or the full-spectrum camera recording at 30 fps in the same area of the same room.

PSL has also utilized a FLIR (forward-looking infrared) camera, which captures thermal images, specifically contrasts in temperatures of objects in the image. While heat signatures can indicate the presence of a living creature, human, rodent or the family pet, unexplained heat signatures have to be explained. Unexplained images of a cold nature are of interest to paranormal investigators, as drops in temperature are often associated with paranormal experiences.

Unexplained phenomena occur in various locations, including many in and around Carthage. To say that paranormal activity does not exist because it has not been fully explained simply begs the ultimate question of why these phenomena occur. After all, five hundred years ago, it was accepted fact that the Earth was flat, and a few hundred years before that, it was accepted that the Earth was the center of the universe. Investigating sites in the context of the history and lives of the people who have lived and died there provides a better understanding of our history as well as the accounts of ghosts witnessed. Is it beyond the realm of possibility that those who died continue to walk among the living? There are many places in Carthage where the past and present intersect, and we never know when and where ghosts are waiting.

BIBLIOGRAPHY

Adams County Union Republican, January 5, 1899.

Banasik, Michael E. "Duty, Honor and Country: The Civil War Experiences of Captain William P. Black, Thirty-Seventh Illinois Infantry." Vol. 6 in *Unwritten Chapters in Civil War West of the River* series. Iowa City, IA: Press of the Camp Pope Bookshop, 2006.

———. *Missouri in 1861: The Civil War Letters of Franc Bangs Wilkie*. Iowa City, IA: Press of the Camp Pope Bookshop, 2001.

Belk, Colleen. *Jasper County, Missouri Tombstones and Civil War Data*. Huntsville, AR: Century Enterprises, 1990.

Bolivar Weekly Courier, April 14, 1860.

Brink-McDonough & Co. *An Illustrated Historical Atlas Map of Jasper County, Missouri*. Philadelphia, 1876.

Brophy, Patrick. *Found No Bushwackers: The 1864 Diary of Sgt. James P. Mallery, Company A, Third Wisconsin Cavalry Stationed at Balltown, Missouri*. Nevada, MO: Vernon County Historical Society, 1988.

———. *Knights of the Bush and Others [Rebels and Yankees]*. Nevada, MO: Vernon County Historical Society, 2005.

Brownlee, Richard S. *Gray Ghosts of the Confederacy: Guerrilla Warfare in the West, 1861–1865*. First Edition. Baton Rouge: Louisiana State University Press, 1958.

Carthage Evening Press. "Bought a Business Block: C.E. Turner Harness & Carriage Co. Make $25,000 Deal; Pay $25,000 for Burlingame & Chaffee Building—Important Changes to Be Made." August 5, 1905.

———. "Brilliant Dance Last Night: Large Gathering at Old Opera House in Honor of Miss Hodges' Guests." February 9, 1900.

Carthage Patriot. "The Ovation: The Carthage Nightingales; An Artist Before the Curtain." April 3, 1878.

Carthage People Press, March 7, 1878.

Carthage Press. "Popular Gathering Place Entering New Era of Service." July 7, 1989.

———. "76 Years a Carthaginian." January 19, 1949.

Cottrell, Steve. *The Battle of Carthage and Carthage in the Civil War*. Carthage, MO: City of Carthage, 1990.

———. *Haunted Ozarks Battlefields: Civil War Ghost Stories and Brief Battle Histories*. First Pelican Edition. Gretna, LA: Pelican Publishing Co., 2010.

Cunningham, Frank. *General Stand Watie's Confederate Indians*. Norman: University of Oklahoma Press, 1998.

1860 Jasper County Slave Census. Carthage: Jasper County, Missouri Records Center Collection.

Garfield County [Enid, OK] Democrat, February 23, 1899.

Gilbert, Joan. *Missouri Ghosts: Spirits, Haunts and Related Lore*. Columbia, MO: Pebble Publishing, 1997.

Gilfillan v. McCrillis. 84 Mo. 576. 1901.

Gilmore, Donald L. *Civil War on the Missouri-Kansas Border*. Gretna, LA: Pelican Publishing Company, Inc., 2006.

Greer, Lillie Johnson. *Through the Years: A History of Peace Church Cemetery: 104 Years/Sherwood Cemetery 100 Years in Galena Township*. N.p., 1961.

Grundy, Arthur. *Art's Scrapbook: Reminisces Over the Years with Arthur Grundy*. Collected works from "Over the Ozarks" column of the Springfield, Missouri *Daily News*. Illustrations by Susie Schaeffer. N.p., 1970.

Hale, Donald R. *They Called Him Bloody Bill: The Life of William Anderson, Missouri Guerrilla, the Missouri Badman Who Taught Jesse James Outlawry*. Clinton, MO: Printery, 1975.

———. *We Rode with Quantrill: Quantrill and the Guerrilla War as Told by the Men Who Were with Him, with a True Sketch of Quantrill's Life*. Clinton, MO: Printery, 1975.

Hansford, Michele Newton. *Images of America: Carthage, Missouri*. Charleston, SC: Arcadia Publishing, 2000.

Harper, Kimberly. *White Man's Heaven: The Lynching and Expulsion of Blacks in the Southern Ozarks, 1894–1909*. Fayetteville: University of Arkansas Press, 2010.

Hinds, Bob. *Ozark Pioneers: Their Trials and Triumphs*. Seventh Printing. Willow Springs, MO: Bob Hinds Books, 2002.

Hinze, David C. *The Battle of Carthage: Border War in Southwest Missouri, July 5, 1861*. First Pelican Printing. Gretna, LA: Pelican Publishing Co., 2004.

James, Larry A. *Pioneers of the Six Bulls: The Newton County, Missouri Saga.* Neosho, MO: Newton County Historical Publications, 1981.

Johnson, Robert Underwood, and Clarence Clough Buel, eds. *Battles and Leaders of the Civil War: Being for the Most Part Contributions of Union and Confederate Officers*. Vol. 1. Boston: Houghton, Mifflin and Co., 1889.

Livingston, John C., Jr. *Such a Foe as Livingston: The Campaign of Confederate Major Thomas R. Livingston's First Missouri Cavalry Battalion of Southwest Missouri*. Wyandotte, OK: Gregath Publishing Company, 2004.

Los Angeles Herald. "The McCrillis Case." January 5, 1899.

———. "The McCrillis Murder: Now on Trial at Carthage, Missouri." December 28, 1898.

McGroarty, John Steven. *Los Angeles from the Mountains to the Sea, with Selected Biography of Actors and Witnesses of the Period of Growth and Achievement.* Chicago: American Historical Society, 1921.

Mills and Company. *History of Jasper County, Missouri: Including a Condensed History of the State, a Complete History of Carthage and Joplin, Other Towns and Townships*. Des Moines, IA: Mills and Company, 1883.

Missouri State Highway Patrol. Introduction to Missouri Historical Society Press edition by Walter A. Schroeder and Howard W. Marshall. *Missouri: The WPA Guide to the "Show Me" State*. New York: Duell, Sloan and Pearce, 1941. Repr., St. Louis: Missouri Historical Society Press, 1998.

Monks, William. *A History of Southern Missouri and Northern Arkansas, Being an Account of the Early Settlements, the Civil War, the Ku-Klux, and Times of Peace.* West Plains, MO: West Plains Journal Co., 1907.

Musick, John R. *Stories of Missouri*. New York: American Book Company, 1897.

O'Donnell, Billy, and Karen Glines. *Painting Missouri: The Counties en Plein Air*. Columbia: University of Missouri Press, 2008.

Offutt, Jason. *Haunted Missouri: A Ghostly Guide to the Show-Me State's Most Spirited Spots*. First Edition. Kirksville, MO: Truman State University Press, 2007.

Randolph, Vance. *Ozark Ghost Stories: Gruesome and Humorous Tales of the Supernatural in the Backwoods of the South*. Photo-Facsimile edition of 1944 Haldeman-Julius Publications edition. Forrest City, AR: Marshall Vance, 1982.

———. *Ozark Magic and Folklore*. New York: Dover Publications, 1964.

Rossiter, Phyllis. *A Living History of the Ozarks*. N.p., n.d.

Schrantz, Ward L. *Jasper County, Missouri, in the Civil War*. Reprint. Originally published 1923. Carthage: Carthage, Missouri Kiwanis Club, 2010.

Shoemaker, Floyd Calvin. *Missouri and Missourians: Land of Contrasts and People of Achievements*. Vol. 1. Chicago, 1943.

Snead, T.L. *The Fight for Missouri, from the Election of Lincoln to the Death of Lyon*. Astor Place, NY: J.J. Little Co., 1886.

Steele, Phillip W., and Steve Cottrell. *Civil War in the Ozarks*. Sixth Printing. Gretna, LA: Pelican Publishing Co., 2003.

Stephens, Mrs. Ann S. *Pictorial History of the War for the Union*. Cincinnati, OH: James R. Hawley Publisher, 1863.

Stevens, Walter Barlow. *Missouri, the Center State: 1821–1915*. 3 vols. Chicago: S.J. Clarke Publishing Co., 1915.

St. Louis Post Everyday Magazine. "Last Hanging in the State of Missouri." March 20, 2001.

Sturges, Judge J.A. *A History of McDonald County, Missouri*. N.p., 1897. Repr., Pineville, MO: McDonald County Public Library, 2003. www.librarymail.org/genehist/sturgesbookv2_2.pdf.

Tremeear, Janice. *Missouri's Haunted Route 66: Ghosts Along the Mother Road*. Charleston, SC: The History Press, 2010.

Vandergriff, Sue. *Then and Now: An Architectural History of the Carthage, Missouri Square and Nearby Structures*. Cassville, MO: Litho Printers & Bindery, 2003.

VanGilder, Marvin L. *Jasper County: The First Two Hundred Years*. Rich Hill, MO: Bell Books, 1995.

Wood, Larry. *The Civil War on the Lower Kansas-Missouri Border*. Second Edition. Joplin, MO: Hickory Press, 2003.

———. *Other Noted Guerrillas of the Civil War in Missouri*. Joplin, MO: Hickory Press, 2007.

Woodruff, W.E. *With the Light Guns in '61–'65: Reminiscences of Eleven Arkansas, Missouri and Texas Light Batteries, in the Civil War*. Little Rock, AR: Central Printing Co., 1903.

WEBSITES

"Community in Conflict: The Impact of the Civil War in the Ozarks." Springfield/Greene County Library and other archives database. www.ozarkscivilwar.org/archives/1140.

Douglas, Julie. "Exploring a Haunted History." Missouri Humanities Council. www.mohumanities.org/news-updates/missouri-passages/november-2010-vol-7-no-9/exploring-a-haunted-history.

"Hootentown: News from the James River." hootentown.wordpress.com/category/missouri/page/5.

Missouri Digital Heritage. www.sos.mo.gov/mdh.

National Park Service, U.S. Department of the Interior. "Military Medicine at Wilson's Creek." www.nps.gov/wicr/historyculture/civil-war-medicine.htm.

———. "Wilson's Creek National Battlefield." www.cr.nps.gov/mwac/wicr_peri/wilsons_creek.htm.

Paranormal Science Lab. www.paranormalsciencelab.com.

———. www.facebook.com/PSLMissouri?ref=hl.

Springfield-Greene County, Missouri online local history collection. Local History. thelibrary.springfield.missouri.org/lochist.

UnitConversion.org.

www.youtube.com/watch?v=-Xfl0m6U8IE.

About the Author

A lifelong resident of Missouri, Lisa Livingston-Martin lives in Webb City. Lisa has practiced law in southwest Missouri for more than twenty years and has long-standing interests in history and the paranormal. She is a co–team leader of Paranormal Science Lab (www.paranormalsciencelab.com), which focuses on paranormal research at historic sites. Lisa is a frequent speaker on the paranormal and the connection between the history of locations and paranormal activity. She graduated from Missouri State University with a BS in political science, later obtaining a JD from Washington University in St. Louis Law School. Lisa is the author of *Civil War Ghosts of Southwest Missouri*, *Haunted Joplin* and *Missouri's Wicked Route 66: Gangsters and Outlaws on the Mother Road*, also published by The History Press.